HAVANA IS
WAITING

AND OTHER PLAYS

HAVANA IS
WAITING

AND OTHER PLAYS

EDUARDO MACHADO

THEATRE COMMUNICATIONS GROUP
NEW YORK
2011

Havana Is Waiting and Other Plays is published by Theatre Communications Group, Inc., 520 Eighth Avenue, 24th Floor, New York, NY 10018-4156

This publication is made possible in part with public funds from the New York State Council on the Arts, a State Agency.

TCG books are exclusively distributed to the book trade by Consortium Book Sales and Distribution.

Library of Congress Cataloging-in-Publication Data
Machado, Eduardo, 1953–
Havana is waiting and other plays / Eduardo Machado.—1st ed.
p. cm.
ISBN 978-1-55936-366-2
1. Cuban Americans--Drama. 2. Cuba--Fiction.
I. Title.
PS3563.A31154H284 2011
812'.54—dc22 2010049626

Book design and composition by Lisa Govan
Cover art: "Isolation" by Gilda Machado-Zimmerling
Cover design by Lisa Govan

First Edition, May 2011

For Michael Domitrovich

Contents

HAVANA IS
WAITING

For my friend, Ed Vassallo

Havana Is Waiting was first produced by the Cherry Lane Theatre (Angelina Fiordellisi, Artistic Director) and opened in 2001. The production was directed by Michael John Garcés; the set design was by Troy Hourie, the costume design was by Elizabeth Hope Clancy, the lighting design was by Kirk Bookman and the sound design was by David Margolin Lawson. The production stage manager was Charles M. Turner III and the stage manager was Karen Munkel. It was performed by:

FEDERICO	Bruce MacVittie
FRED	Ed Vassallo
ERNESTO	Felix Solis
DRUMMER	Richard Marquez

An earlier version of *Havana Is Waiting* (then called *When the Sea Drowns in Sand*) premiered in the 2001 Humana Festival at Actors Theatre of Louisville. The production was directed by Michael John Garcés; the set design was by Neil Patel, the costume design was by Lindsay W. Davis, the lighting design was by Tony Penna and the sound design was by Martin Desjardins. The stage manager was Charles M. Turner, III. It was performed by:

FEDERICO	Joseph Urla
FRED	Ed Vassallo
ERNESTO	Felix Solis
DRUMMER	Hugh "Fuma" Petersen

CHARACTERS

FEDERICO, a man in his forties

FRED, an American-Italian in his early thirties

ERNESTO, a taxi driver in his thirties

AN AFRO-CUBAN DRUMMER

PLACE

New York City and Havana, Cuba. The set is abstract and is a dark blue. The set pieces are minimal. When they are in a car or plane there are no seats. The drummer is onstage. The feeling should be of someone in a dream.

TIME

1999

Act One

Scene 1

Lights up on Federico, a man in his forties. He seems to be suspended in the air; all we see is his face. Drums play. He chants and talks.

FEDERICO *(Chants)*:
> I land there.
> I see it,
> the world fills me sweetly.
> Ah. Ah. Ah.
> Enraptured
> in such a precarious
> dream.
> Can it be? Is this me?
> Ah
> ah
> ah.
> I'm loose now,
> I choose now
> to be with you darling.

Don't dangle the future
no meaning in that.
I'm captured in a rapturous
rhapsody.
Ah
ah
ah
aah.
It's me, dear.
I'm home now,
I'm free now,
to be just
like me now.
Oh darling
in Spanish
don't speak more in English
no meaning in that,
ay
ay
ay aaay.
When you've reached
your promised land.
Where the people often dance.
Oh
oh
oh,
Aguántame cariño,
¿eres dulce mi vida?
¡Soy yo, amor!
No llores,
¡Llegué a mi hogar! ¿Estoy en mi hogar?
Mi casa
¿mi casa?
¿Estoy en mi casa?
¡No! No casa.
¡No!
¡Ay!

¡Ay! ¡Ay!
No . . .
No home.
It's all lost
my darling
you left me.
Like I always knew you would.
Why am I not any good?
Why can't I hold onto you?
Or it?
Or her?
Or me?
I'm beginning to awake now
like I always new I would.
The sun shines
in bed now and
alone.
Still so far away from home.
Ay, No!
Oh!
Ah, ah!
My eyes clear
I focus.
And I see
I'm all alone.
Should I just get up and pee?
Why do good things come in dreams?
Alone now,
no home now.
And for sure
I know you left me.
Like I always knew you would.
Like I always knew you would.
Like I always knew you would.
¿Qué pasa? ¿Qué pasa? ¿Qué pasa?

(We hear his own voice echoing back to him.)

FEDERICO'S VOICE *(Offstage)*: What's going on? What's going on! What's going on?

FEDERICO: That's not how I would have translated it. I would have said, "What's doing?" No that's not it. "How does it go!" No, too casual. "How am I?" Too psychological. "How are you doing?" Too many words. Some things are impossible to translate. God, if two words are impossible to translate, how do you translate an entire life? *¿Qué pasa?* "What's happening?" Too black, too street, too '70s. But that's the closest to my original meaning I think. "What's happening." Fred, what's happening?

(Lights change. He is no longer flying. Federico is sitting onstage.
     Fred, an American-Italian in his early thirties, enters with a video camera in his hand and a suitcase.)

FRED: The car is waiting.

FEDERICO: What?

FRED: We are going to Cuba, today.

FEDERICO: I got my visa?

FRED: They faxed it last night at the last moment. Remember?

FEDERICO: That wasn't a dream?

FRED: No.

FEDERICO: I thought it was a dream.

FRED: Come on, you got your passport and your visa. It only took five years.

FEDERICO: Right. You think they'll let me in?

FRED: Yes, of course.

FEDERICO: I can go back?

FRED: Yes. I'm so glad I'm going with you. We are going to Cuba!

FEDERICO: When we are at the airport tell them we are going to Cancun!

FRED: Right.

FEDERICO: I got my Cuban passport, my visa. I got my heart in my stomach. I hope I don't vomit. I got my memories, my past. I hope they're not all destroyed. What if they don't let me in?

FRED: The car is waiting.

FEDERICO: No.

FRED: What?

FEDERICO: No. I'm not going.

FRED: What do you mean? You've been waiting for this.

FEDERICO: No, I can't go, no I can't do it. It's too late. A year ago maybe, not now. No!

FRED: Federico—

FEDERICO: Where's my dog?

FRED: I don't know. Who cares about the dog?

FEDERICO: I care!

FRED: Jesus fucking Christ!

FEDERICO: Stella!

FRED: Since when?

FEDERICO: Stella baby! Stella, come to daddy. Daddy needs you.

FRED: Stop stalling. Federico!

FEDERICO: Stella. I need you! Who's going to take care of my dog!?

(Stella starts to bark; she is under the bed.)

FRED: We arranged for a student to take care of the dog.

FEDERICO: Daddy's joining you. Come here, bitch.

(Federico tries to crawl under the bed. Fred holds onto to him.)

Let go of me!

FRED: No!

FEDERICO: Getting rough aren't you.

FRED: Isn't that how you like it?

FEDERICO: How would you know?

FRED: I can figure you out.

FEDERICO: Aren't you straight?

FRED: Of course I am . . .

FEDERICO: Then why do you think about what I'm like in bed?

FRED: Well, I'm . . .

FEDERICO: Yeah?

FRED: I can imagine . . .

FEDERICO: So you imagine what I'm like in bed?

FRED: Wait. You're trying to change the subject. Listen Federico—

FEDERICO: What, Fred? Tell me Fred!

FRED: We are getting on a plane and we are going to take you home.

FEDERICO: You're not my father, you're not my mother, you're not my lover. You're on your own.

FRED: Stop it! I'm your friend. I'm not gonna let you go with that asshole.

FEDERICO: Touché.

FRED: Yeah.

FEDERICO: Yeah? Underneath the bed with the dog, that's the only home I want, know or need. Or can handle. Stella, come out here and save me. Bite him, Stella, bite him. Stella, you love me don't you?

FRED: See.

FEDERICO: What?

FRED: She won't come out. I care more about you than she does.

FEDERICO: Then forget about the trip . . . all this . . . fucking . . . self-help crap. There is no closure. Sometimes there is no closure!

FRED: Yes there is!

FEDERICO: The terror. Do you know the terror?

FRED: I'm willing to get on a plane for you.

FEDERICO: What?

FRED: Even though I am terrified.

FEDERICO: Go home! Yankee, go home.

FRED: I have a fear of flying, you know that. Haven't been on a plane in two years. Since that take off from Denver, I kept reading your anthology. That's what kept me alive I swear. This fear is real for me! I drive everywhere. But no, fucking Cuba you can't drive to. You gotta get there through the longest routes imaginable. Eight hours when it should be three. Eight hours on three different planes. That's how much I care about you!

FEDERICO: Yeah and it's your country that started an embargo.

FRED: What?

FEDERICO: That's why it takes so long to get there, the embargo. Your country's embargo.

FRED: It's your relatives in Miami that keep it going.

FEDERICO: Yeah, so?

FRED: We planned it. Let's do it.

FEDERICO: Do it?

FRED: Yeah.

FEDERICO: Why should I trust you?

FRED: You're my buddy. I'm your buddy.

FEDERICO: I have too many buddies.

FRED: Why are you so undecided?

FEDERICO: Fred, I told this story too many times, to too many people. So many that by now it should have lost all its meaning, but it hasn't. Did they throw me out, or did I walk out. Was I abandoned or did I set myself free? I do not know the answer to that. Was I thrown out, or did I walk away from my country? Did I decide to leave, or was I tricked?

FRED: I don't know, Federico.

FEDERICO: I don't either. There is an airport in Havana where I learned the meaning of impotence. I saw my mother on the other side of the glass. She let me go on a plane without her. It could have been forever. I held my brother's hand. I was nine, he was six. I handed over my blue aquamarine ring to the militia. My brother wet his pants. My father did not reassure us. They searched my butthole for diamonds. My brother sucked his thumb. And the world spinned around in the opposite direction and the wind carried us away.

FRED: It's gonna be okay.

FEDERICO: And I floated. Without a voice . . . nothing was recognizable. And I made up somebody new. And I survived.

FRED: Beautifully . . .

FEDERICO: What?

FRED: I think you survived beautifully.

FEDERICO: That little boy with the militia prodding his ass. That's what's waiting for me. Back there . . . down there in Havana. That's home. You want me to get on a plane and go back and face that.

FRED: Yes.

FEDERICO: You sadist!

FRED: It's what you need.

FEDERICO: Yes, I do.

FRED: Good.

FEDERICO: Help me. Okay, buddy?

FRED: Get dressed.

FEDERICO: Someone will take care of my dog?

(Federico starts getting dressed.)

FRED: Your concern over your dog is highly hypocritical.

FEDERICO: I care about the dog. I mean Stella doesn't care about me. But I have a . . . I don't know, a need to be abused by her.

FRED: Who abuses who in that relationship is questionable.

FEDERICO: I feed her everyday. I take care of her. No one takes care of me that way.

FRED: I will, bitch.

FEDERICO: I like it when you talk rough. Oh God. Fred!

FRED: It's time.

FEDERICO: Yeah.

FRED: Yeah.

FEDERICO: Are you sure?

FRED: Trust me.

(Blackout.)

SCENE 2

Federico and Fred are flying. Fred is sleeping. Drums.

FEDERICO: Everyone seems to know I had to go. Wish you well. Now go! Go home. Home is that sentimental abstract place. Home is that yearning in your gut feeling. Cut down at nine. A gulf more potent than any Berlin Wall. Separated. So now I sit in a plane. I check my passport, my Cuban passport! My birth certificate. My identity? My identity . . . flamboyant writer, professor . . . Blah, blah, blah. Darling to some, a monster to others. No doubt about his talent. His talent is questionable. Savior of peoples' creative life. Horrible husband, lover, and wife! Good friend, abandons all his friends. New Yorker from L.A. . . . my identity. But on this plane. Back home. Home to where there is no home. Or is the air home? I cried in the bathroom, because I've begun to recall another person that was me. And my friend Fred sleeps. On a plane towards who knows . . . December 1, 1999. 9:15 P.M. Eastern time.

(Blackout.)

Scene 3

Cuba. Fred lights a cigarette. Federico takes it from him. Fred lights another one.

FRED: God bless a country where you can smoke anywhere. Amen! Even in the elevators. Cuban cigarettes are heaven. Amen.

FEDERICO: Is it that one? Or that one?

(Ernesto, a taxi driver in his thirties, walks in. He is carrying a rag.)

ERNESTO: I don't know. You used to live here, not me. I got a kid to watch the car.

FRED: You parked it?

ERNESTO: Yeah. In front of the first place he thought was his house.

FEDERICO: Have I forgotten where my house is? I swore to myself I'd never forget. I stayed up at night for years trying to remember it.

FRED: You okay?

ERNESTO: Should we get back in my car?

FEDERICO: Happiest day of my life.

FRED: Good.

(Fred opens a small pillbox filled with Valiums and downs a Valium.)

FEDERICO: You okay?

FRED: Happiest day of your life.

FEDERICO: Right, then why are you downing a Valium?

FRED: That's why we brought them.

FEDERICO: Right. Do you understand us, Manny? Manny?

FRED: His name is Ernesto.

FEDERICO: Ernesto? Really?

FRED: Jesus.

FEDERICO: So Manny, Ernesto, so?

ERNESTO: You're happy, why shouldn't you be, you're home?

(Lights switch.)

FEDERICO *(Chants)*:

> Not real
> walking into
> What?
> The car is burgundy,
> my blood is blue.
> What am I to do!
> Oh God!
> The water is blue
> the sky is cloudy
> it might rain,
> like I always knew
> it would.
> The town
> my town
> is still here.
> Is the house
> in the distance?
> You waited
> like I always knew you would.

ERNESTO: So you went on the Peter Pan flights?

(Federico does not answer.)

FRED: He was only nine, by himself with his six-year-old brother.

ERNESTO: What's his name?

FRED: I never met his brother and I don't know his name.

ERNESTO: And you two seem so close.

FRED: Oh we are . . .

ERNESTO: I thought so.

FRED: . . . But his brother lives in another state. So does mine, and he doesn't know my brother or my brother's name.

FEDERICO: Al. That's your brother's name.

FRED: So you know his name. But he doesn't know my brother.

FEDERICO: Jesus.

FRED: What?

FEDERICO: My brother's name is Jesus. He was born on Christmas day.

ERNESTO: Tragedy.

FRED: Really?

ERNESTO: Shameful.

FRED: What.

ERNESTO: So many kids, thirteen thousand. Sent to the U.S. Like cattle, all because of a C.I.A. plot and an English woman living here in Cuba. She was a spy, when she got old the C.I.A. sent her a wheelchair. She died here.

FRED: In La Habana?

ERNESTO: Yes. Like she was one of us.

FEDERICO: Was her name Wendy?

ERNESTO: I don't know. But my friend made a documentary abut it. The people in it, the children now grown up. Were broken by the experience. You can tell when you watch the documentary. Fidel should have stopped their immigration. But he gave them a special kind of visa. Always trying to please, Fidel. Back then. He wanted to please.

FEDERICO: That's not what my parents thought.

ERNESTO: Gave you the visa, didn't he?

FEDERICO: To get rid of us.

ERNESTO: No. When those thirteen thousand kids left. We cried.

FEDERICO: We all cried.

FRED: I'd like to see that documentary. Would you, Federico?

FEDERICO: I lived it, Fred.

FRED: Oh.

ERNESTO: So many children, C.I.A. plot. Destroy the child, corrupt the revolution. Pity.

FEDERICO: This is not the block. This is not my block. Fuck, I thought I could find it. Fuck.

ERNESTO: Maybe someone remembers your family here. What did they do?

FEDERICO: We owned the bus company.

ERNESTO: Then they got to remember. They rode the busses. Paid you a nickel everyday. People don't forget that.

FEDERICO: Really?

ERNESTO: I'll ask someone that looks old and they'll remember.

FRED: Yeah. We'll find it, baby. We'll find it.

FEDERICO: Wait a minute. The address is on my birth certificate.

FRED: Really?

FEDERICO: I was born here, Fred.

FRED: I know.

FEDERICO: And I've come back.

FRED: I'm so proud of you.

ERNESTO: I'm very happy that we started this period of "family reconciliation."

FRED AND FEDERICO: What?

ERNESTO: That's the period Fidel said we are in now. That's why he's letting you all come back.

FRED: Really?

ERNESTO: Yes.

FEDERICO: I think it should be called the period of "dollar reconciliation."

ERNESTO: That's true.

(They laugh.)

FRED: I'm proud of you.

FEDERICO: Why?

FRED: That you can laugh about it. Although it would be all right with me if you cried.

(Federico grabs the pillbox from Fred's hand and takes a Valium.)

FEDERICO: Want one?
ERNESTO: Valium, yes.
FRED: Valium yes, Yankee no!

(Ernesto laughs nervously. He takes the Valium with his hand. Ernesto takes out his wallet and very carefully stores the Valium in it. Then he puts the wallet in his pocket.)

FEDERICO: You really do believe in saving for the future.
ERNESTO: We have to.
FEDERICO: So simple: "We have to."
FRED: You okay?
FEDERICO: Don't I look it!
FRED: Sure.
FEDERICO: Good.
FRED: Now take out your birth certificate.
FEDERICO: Why?
FRED: So we can find the address.
FEDERICO: Right.

(Federico searches through his pockets.)

God!
FRED: You lost it?
FEDERICO: No . . .
FRED: Then where is it?
ERNESTO: It certainly is a beautiful little town. My wife and I used to come here.
FEDERICO: If you and your wife used to come here, then why can't you find my goddamn house!
ERNESTO: . . . We used to come here every . . .
FRED: Is it in your wallet?
ERNESTO: . . . summer. We had big barbecues down on the beach . . . Perfect beach town only fifteen minutes from the center of La Habana . . . Barbecues by the beach, fish, sometimes lobster.

I know a man who sells lobster for dollars. He's watched. Still does it, under the table. If you want to make a meal I can get you a good price on lobster, fresh fish, right out of the Gulf. He sells them out of his garage. If you want to buy, I'll get it for you.

FRED: You lost it.

FEDERICO: What?

FRED: You lost it.

FEDERICO: Give me that.

ERNESTO: He also sells those antennas, which are against the law, because you can get stations from everywhere in the world! But people buy them, hide them, and use them. What are they called? They're round and . . .

FRED: Satellite dishes?

ERNESTO: Yes.

FRED: Satellite dishes, yes?

ERNESTO: I want to make enough money to buy a satellite dish.

FEDERICO: Name names.

ERNESTO: That's not funny.

FRED: People name names?

ERNESTO: Yes. Like with everything there's good and bad.

FRED: They do in America also.

ERNESTO: I know blacklisting . . . McCarthy . . . Black Panthers . . . Shame.

FRED: And other things.

ERNESTO: You have a right to be anything but a communist, in your country.

FRED: Among other things.

(Federico goes back to looking for his birth certificate. He has taken many pieces of paper out of his pocket.)

FEDERICO: Passport. List of people to contact. Airplane tickets. Mom's cousin's address. Picture of what the house looked like in 1959 . . . traveler's checks . . . cash . . .

FRED: Keep the cash where it is.

FEDERICO: Fine. Where the fuck is the birth certificate?

FRED: You'll find it. Keep looking through that money belt. *(To Ernesto)* How come you can afford a car?

ERNESTO: I made ten thousand dollars. Can you believe it, ten thousand dollars?

FRED: You did?

FEDERICO: How?

ERNESTO: I sculpt.

FEDERICO: Ah.

ERNESTO: Special kind of sculpting from broken glass. Never been done the way I do it. I showed in Paris last year.

FRED: Great.

FEDERICO: Paris wow. You got to go to Paris.

ERNESTO: Sold this sculpting to an Italian restaurant that is opening in La Habana. That's how I bought the car.

(Ernesto and Fred look down the street and admire the car.)

1949 Chevy.

FRED: Beauty.

ERNESTO: I'll show you a picture of my sculpting when we get back to the house.

FRED: Can't wait. I'll take a picture with my camera. A picture of the picture so I can show it to my friends on the web. This camera is digital. Goes straight into my computer.

ERNESTO: You know anybody who owns restaurants?

FRED: My father knows people.

ERNESTO: There's a way that they can buy my fountains through a Paris gallery, on their web site.

FEDERICO: Visa bill, Visa bill. Visa bill.

FRED: I'll help you in any way I can.

ERNESTO: Yes? Thank you, Fred. I made ten thousand dollars. That's how I bought the car. Great. The car is paying for itself. By driving friends like you around. Twenty dollars a day. Everybody wins. Right, Fred?

FRED: Yeah. I'm Fred. He's Federico.

ERNESTO: Thank God you are not both called Federico.

FRED: Actually my name is Federico, people just call me Fred.

FEDERICO: And when I was first here. I mean over there. I was called Fred.

FRED: Maybe I should go back to Federico.

ERNESTO: No, you're not Cuban.

FRED: Federico is Italian also. And I am of Italian . . . my grandparents were Italian. Immigrants. But they called me Fred, 'cause that was the thing to do in Queens.

FEDERICO: I found it!

FRED: Good. I knew you would.

FEDERICO: 330 Maceo.

ERNESTO: 330 Maceo. I know that man there sitting on his porch. I'll ask him for directions.

FEDERICO: Thank you, Manny . . .

ERNESTO: Ernesto.

FEDERICO: Thank you, Ernesto.

ERNESTO: Take care of your man.

FRED: What?

ERNESTO: It's hard to come back home.

(Ernesto walks away.)

FRED: Is it?

FEDERICO: I don't know.

FRED: I think he thinks I'm your boy.

FEDERICO: I'll set him straight.

FRED: I don't care, Papi.

FEDERICO: Uh huh. I don't believe you.

FRED: I don't!

FEDERICO: Don't get defensive.

FRED: No?

FEDERICO: No. I'm not accusing you of anything.

FRED: Are you sure?

FEDERICO: Yes.

FRED: We're just friends?

FEDERICO: Yes.

FRED: Good.

FEDERICO: The water is blue, the palm trees sway. I can taste salt on my lips. You'd think I've been crying. But it's because we are surrounded by the sea.

FRED: It's okay with me if you cry.

FEDERICO: But not with me.

FRED: He's talking to that man for a long time.

FEDERICO: The man is black.

FRED: Handsome.

FEDERICO: You like black men. Don't you?

FRED: I don't like men.

FEDERICO: But, I've noticed, that you always notice black men.

FRED: Hey!

FEDERICO: I'm teasing you.

FRED: The only man I am interested in is you. This. I need to see you through this.

FEDERICO: Thanks. Mamá. The water is blue. The mud is red. The palm trees still sway. What I dreamt of all my life. Coming back to "Neverland." The sand will be white. And there's a volcano inside of me. A volcano called regret. That I cannot let go of, Fred. I cannot . . .

FRED: Federico?

FEDERICO: What?

FRED: I had an impulse to do something cheap.

FEDERICO: What.

FRED: Repeating the volcano bit back to you as you said it.

FEDERICO: Don't quote me please.

FRED: Can I turn on the camera?

FEDERICO: Well.

FRED: Please.

FEDERICO: Sure.

(Fred turns on the camera. Federico imitates Blanche DuBois.)

FRED: "What's the matter honey, are you lost?"

FEDERICO: "They told me to take a street car named Desire and then transfer to one called Cemetery, and ride six blocks and get off at Elysian Fields."

FRED: "That's where you are now."

FEDERICO: "At Elysian Fields?"

FRED: "This here is Elysian Fields."

FEDERICO: "They must have not understood what number I wanted."

FRED: "What number are you looking for?"

FEDERICO: "632."

FRED: "You don't have to look no further."

FEDERICO: "I'm looking for my sister Stella DuBois. I mean Mrs. Stanley Kowalski."

(They laugh. Federico takes the camera and Fred imitates Blanche.)

What's the matter are you lost honey?

FRED: I took a Mexican airlines flight to Mexico City. And then transferred to one that took me to Cancun. Walked six blocks till I got to Air Caribe, got on that one, a plane with no windows. To land here.

FEDERICO: What number are you looking for?

FRED: 330 Maceo.

(They laugh. Fred takes the camera, points it at Federico.)

So what does it feel like?

FEDERICO: Like having your pupils replaced and you can see again. Like walking into fiction, like being born again in the eyes of Fidel. There's a black hole inside of me . . .

FRED: I thought it was a volcano?

FEDERICO: It's dripping out little red drops of ink. Not of blood because my blood is blue. Little drops of ink. For all the ways that I betrayed my country with a pen.

FRED: Yeah?

FEDERICO: Yeah.

FRED: You didn't betray them.

FEDERICO: I did.

FRED: No.

FEDERICO: Really?

FRED: Yes.

FEDERICO: How would you know?

FRED: I know.

FEDERICO: How could you know what it's like?

FRED: Tell me.

FEDERICO: Shut the camera.

FRED: No.

FEDERICO: If you don't shut the camera, I won't tell you.

FRED: Why?

FEDERICO: Because that's how things are.

FRED: Really.

FEDERICO: With me.

FRED: But . . .

FEDERICO: No. No buts. I won't.

FRED: Come on.

FEDERICO: Some things are private.

FRED: Whatever.

FEDERICO: Some things are just for you and me.

FRED: Sorry, baby.

FEDERICO: I don't know, it's dangerous, Fred. I am beginning to feel like I am someone. That I belong. That someone loves me.

FRED: People love you.

FEDERICO: That my people love me.

FRED: I'm your people. Aren't I your people?

FEDERICO: No.

FRED: Well, fuck you!

FEDERICO: You are a nice stranger that I met.

FRED: How can you!

FEDERICO: It's not the same.

FRED: That hurts.

FEDERICO: Sorry.

FRED: That hurts. I don't feel like you are a stranger to me. And believe me, you are not nice. I'm . . . I'm putting it out here for you.

FEDERICO: Are you?

FRED: Yes. Yes I am.

FEDERICO: With me?

FRED: Yes.

FEDERICO: I can't trust that.

FRED: Why not?

FEDERICO: You usually run away.

FRED: What?

FEDERICO: We usually get close and then you run away.

FRED: That's not true.

FEDERICO: You know it's true, Fred.

FRED: I won't this time.

FEDERICO: Why not? What's different?

FRED: Well . . .

FEDERICO: Tell me Fred. Hm?

FRED: Because I'm the one. That saw your face. When you went home.

FEDERICO: If we find it.

FRED: Home to Cuba. I've already seen it. So has my camera. So I have proof. Proof that Freddie did go home.

FEDERICO: We'll see.

FRED: You will.

FEDERICO: I hope he got directions.

(Ernesto enters.)

ERNESTO: I know the way.

FEDERICO: Where?

ERNESTO: Up and down that hill.

FEDERICO: Up and down that hill? Impossible.

ERNESTO: Apparently you didn't keep it all up there like you thought.

FEDERICO: What?

ERNESTO: The directions.

FRED: Well, thirty-eight years is thirty-eight years.

ERNESTO: Yes, it is.

FEDERICO: Let's get in the car.

FRED: Right.

ERNESTO: Listen.

FRED: What?

ERNESTO: Good thing that I have friends in this town.

FRED: You can say that again.

FEDERICO: Is it still standing? Did he tell you.

ERNESTO: It's a school now.

FEDERICO: Of course it's still standing. My father's cousin was here last year. He said it was still standing. Let's get in the car.

(Ernesto looks upset.)

ERNESTO: Do we have to?

FRED: What's wrong, Ernesto?

ERNESTO: I'm so sorry.

FEDERICO: They tore it down?

ERNESTO: No, that's not it.

FRED: What?

ERNESTO: The car.

FEDERICO: I didn't expect to find the cars, or the buses. Though the way people fix things around here. The buses are probably still running.

ERNESTO: No, my car.

FEDERICO: I bet that car was left by some family that went to Miami. I bet they have a picture of it. Up on their wall.

FRED: What's wrong with the car?

ERNESTO: You heard it, Fred?

FRED: Sure, I heard it. Yeah! What?

ERNESTO: Misfiring, right? I have to clean the spark plugs or we won't get anywhere. Fucking Russian spark plugs.

FRED: Russian spark plugs in a 1940s Chevy. Next time I come I'm bringing American spark plugs.

FEDERICO: You already decided that you are coming back.

FRED: Haven't you?

FEDERICO: No.

ERNESTO: Please Fred, bring us real spark plugs, Fred.

FRED: I will.

ERNESTO: I gotta clean the spark plugs.

FEDERICO: You know, I love cars. We owned a fleet. Of cabs and buses. We ruled this land with our automobiles.

ERNESTO: It's gonna take a few minutes. Take a walk. See more of your town.

FEDERICO: I want to see. *Mi casa.*

FRED: "*Mi casa*," my home. Right?

FEDERICO: Right, Fred.

FRED: See, I am learning Spanish.

FEDERICO: Before you know it, you are going to be Cuban.

FRED: I know.

ERNESTO: Well, he is Cuban by injection.

FRED: What do you mean by that?

ERNESTO: Well, the rum you've been drinking. Dark, aged and one hundred percent Cuban. Right, Federico?

FEDERICO: Right, Manny.

FRED: Ernesto.

FEDERICO: Ernesto, right.

FRED: Listen, Ernesto . . .

ERNESTO: Federico and Fred. I still can't get over it.

FEDERICO: Our towels have "F and F" intertwining. "F and F" embroidered on them.

FRED: Stop it!

FEDERICO: I thought you didn't care.

FRED: I'm going to take a walk.

(Fred leaves.)

FEDERICO: I'm staying.

ERNESTO: It's going to be a few minutes.

FEDERICO: I need a few minutes.

(Ernesto leaves.)

Close your eyes and breathe, breathe it in.

(Fred walks by Federico and pats his shoulder. Federico holds onto his hand.)

Don't go. Don't be mad.

FRED: I'm not. I don't care.

FEDERICO: I don't want to betray you.

FRED: I won't let you. Thanks.

FEDERICO: My father betrayed my mother. My father always betrayed my mother.

FRED: So did mine.

FEDERICO: Yes?

FRED: Yes.

FEDERICO: We left our country. Betrayed it. This. Her.

FRED: You think this country is a woman?

FEDERICO: Yes. Then we betrayed each other. But once . . . the first time it became crystal clear was on Valentine's Day. They had just gotten to the U.S. We were in L.A. . . . We were poor. My mother made a heart-shaped cake. Not any regular kind. Not out of mix. But the kind that is mostly eggs and a little bit of flour.

FRED: Sponge cake.

FEDERICO: Yes, from scratch. Then she poured syrup . . . drowned it in syrup. The kind that has a little bit of rum . . .

FRED: Dark rum or white rum?

FEDERICO: White, exiled Bacardi rum.

FRED: Yum.

FEDERICO: My mother made a heart-shaped cake and decorated it with white and pink meringues . . . little roses all around its edges. And in the middle she wrote "Gilda and Othon." And waited for him. He came home with carnations, yellow and white. She presented him with the cake. He shoved it to the side of the table. Shoved it to the side of the table without even looking at it. Without a kiss. Without a thank you, just a half-embarrassed smile. And it confirmed to me that he did not love us. I suspected it because he took me away from this. This town. My town.

ERNESTO: Okay. We are going to walk to your house.

FEDERICO: What?

ERNESTO: My friend will watch the car. It's only up and down the hill. Fred. I think those spark plugs, if we are lucky, will take us back to La Habana. But they are not going to start and stop and start again. I don't want to turn it on and then turn it off.

FRED: What?

ERNESTO: The car.

FRED: I see.

FEDERICO: Waste of twenty dollars.

FRED: No! We'll walk up and down the hill.

ERNESTO: That sounds better.

FRED: Yeah.

FEDERICO: Let's go.

ERNESTO: To find your childhood.

FRED: That's why we're here.

(They walk. Federico starts to puts things back into his money belt. He holds his birth certificate.)

FEDERICO: Fred.

FRED: Excited?

FEDERICO: Yes.

FRED: Good.

FEDERICO: I think you should have this?

FRED: What?

FEDERICO: You know where you are going, right Manuel?

FRED: Ernesto!

FEDERICO: Ernesto, right.

ERNESTO: 330 Maceo, up and down the hill.

FEDERICO: So take it.

FRED: Your birth certificate?

FEDERICO: Yes.

FRED: Why don't you put it back in your money belt?

FEDERICO: Because I have too many things in it already.

(Federico stuffs things into it.)

My glasses. Credit cards. Take it, I have a feeling I'm going to lose something.

FRED: Your soul?

FEDERICO: I thought that's what I was going to find.

ERNESTO: Here's the hill.

FEDERICO: Here, take my passport also.

FRED: Your entire identity?

ERNESTO: That's love.

FEDERICO: No, I still have my green card.

FRED: Your entire Cuban identity?

ERNESTO: That's *amore*.

FEDERICO: And I'm keeping the traveler's checks and the cash and the credit cards.

ERNESTO: Are they American credit cards?

FEDERICO: Yes.

ERNESTO: They don't work here.

FEDERICO: Take the passport, Fred, and stop being a baby.

FRED: Aren't I your baby?

ERNESTO: European and Canadian and Latin-American and Asian and Japanese and Australian credit cards work here. They don't have an embargo with us.

FRED: We know.

FEDERICO: Here.

ERNESTO: But they do in the U.S.A . . .

FRED: It's a big responsibility. A person's identity.

FEDERICO: I want it in your big capable hands.

FRED: Well.

(Fred takes the papers.)

FEDERICO: Thank you.

FRED: Reluctantly I take them.

(Fred focuses his camera and points it at Federico.)

ERNESTO: We are on top of the hill. Look down, does anything look familiar?

FEDERICO: Yes and no?

FRED: Yes and no? Did you hear that, folks?

FEDERICO: You're going to have that thing on! Are you!

FRED: You'll be glad I did later on.

ERNESTO: That's love.

FEDERICO: Yes.

FRED: Friendship.

FEDERICO: It's the dearest kind of love.

FRED: Yes, it is.

FEDERICO: Absolutely.

ERNESTO: But not the most passionate.

(Fred brushes Federico's hair with his hand.)

FRED: Little boy lost.

FEDERICO: You're messing up my hair.

FRED: You don't care.

FEDERICO: No . . . little boy lost, looking for my own home. Should I fly in the window? And take away all the little school children? That have little desks in what used to be my bedroom. And tell them, "We are flying to Hialeah, then L.A., then New York. Your little selves will always be here but . . ."

FRED: Look out the window. Do you remember?

FEDERICO: I don't know. "Your little selves will always be here. But your voice will turn into something you won't recognize."

FRED: Walk into it.

FEDERICO: The past.

FRED: It's right in front of you.

FEDERICO: It's always been in front of me.

FRED: Yeah. But now it exists. Still here. Waiting for you.

FEDERICO: No.

FRED: Yes.

FEDERICO: Breathe.

FRED: Yes.

ERNESTO: I hope we are walking the right way.

FRED: Take my hand.

FEDERICO: Your strong hand?

FRED: Yes.

FEDERICO: My mother's beige skirt, it swayed in the breeze . . . My brother's red tricycle . . . his birthday cake that looked like a Christmas tree covered with snow, but the snow was really shredded coconut . . . my cousin's horses! Oh my God! I remember looking at this street corner from above. As I rode with my cousin on his horse . . . Held onto him, I was five . . . on his horse. Oh my God!

FRED: You okay?

FEDERICO: Are we near it?

ERNESTO: Are we?

FEDERICO: I think so. Light me a cig. Will you, Fred?

FRED: Yeah.

(Fred lights a cigarette. Federico doesn't take it.)

FEDERICO: Walking . . . marbles. We played marbles on this street corner. That's the house!

FRED: Where?

FEDERICO: There.

(Fred points his camera.)

ERNESTO: Okay.

FEDERICO: No . . . that's the Marqueses' house. The one that always had a Rolls in the driveway. Oh my God if they saw it now. It's faded.

(Fred places the cigarette in Federico's hand.)

FRED: Here.

FEDERICO: Inhale, exhale.

(Federico smokes. Fred focuses his camera.)

ERNESTO: Exciting, the period of "family reconciliation."

FEDERICO: Inhale, exhale. Look across the street.

FRED: Action.

FEDERICO: Let the smoke fill your lungs, want to die, want to live.

FRED: Camera on!

FEDERICO: It's across the street.

ERNESTO: That is the one?

FEDERICO: I need to . . . I need a minute.

FRED: He needs to walk there slowly.

FEDERICO: Yeah, let me have another cig.

FRED: Love this country, you can smoke anywhere.

ERNESTO: Good. I'll go see if they'll let you in.

FRED: Good.

ERNESTO: Yeah. Can I have a cigarette?

FRED: Sure.

ERNESTO: I'll light it on my own, thank you.

FRED: Sure.

(Ernesto starts to walk away.)

Can I film there?

ERNESTO: Stay over here and use your zoom lens.

FRED: But . . .

ERNESTO: It'll be better.

FEDERICO: Why? It's my house!

ERNESTO: Was.

FEDERICO: Was my house, right.

ERNESTO: Federico and Fred . . .

FRED: Funny, isn't it.

(Ernesto walks away.)

God you heard the ocean every night when you were a little kid.

FEDERICO: What?

FRED: The ocean, can't you hear it?

FEDERICO: The ocean is all the way down the hill.

FRED: So?

FEDERICO: I never heard it from my window.

FRED: Listen.

FEDERICO: I don't hear it.

FRED: I do, it's calling me.

FEDERICO: I have to slowly walk into my house.

FRED: Yes, you do. Walk in now.

FEDERICO: Yes, right.

FRED: Can I film you?

FEDERICO: Yes. My mother will like it.

FRED: We'll make a little movie afterward.

FEDERICO: After I walk in, just follow me with the camera. Fuck them.

(Federico exits offstage. Fred points his camera.)

FRED *(Narrating what he's filming)*: When they let you in. I'll follow. He walks slowly down the street, he inhales one long deep drag. Ernesto is talking to a black woman. She has a mulatto baby, a girl with frizzy brown hair, lacy pink underwear, no shirt, and white dress shoes. The mulatto baby is playing on the steps like he did. Like you did, Federico. See that. He walks towards the entrance. His hand trembles a little. He looks towards what used to be the rose garden. He says, "That used to be . . ." Ernesto stops him and smiles. He's talking to the woman. She shakes her head no. He walks towards the door. She stops him. They argue. He's pleading. She shakes her head. No. Fuck, they're not going to let him in. He goes to the big window, he opens a shutter and looks in. Are you finding it. What you're looking for? Your heart, that's what you're looking for. I hope you find it 'cause then you can help me to find mine. I know it's in here somewhere inside my house, my body. He's moved away from the window. They smile at him, he smiles at them. He tells a joke. They all laugh. He tickles the baby's chin. The baby smiles. Now he is going to the left side of the house. The house. He points at me. Let me zoom in. He's looking inside a smaller window . . . he mouths to me, "My room." Fly in, Freddie! Fly in. He looks away. There's a small tear in his eye. He wipes it away. He smiles at the camera. Let's see what Ernesto is doing. Offering the woman a cig. So he does own a pack. She takes it. He lights it. They whisper something to each other. Federico is walking up to them. He shakes hands with the woman. They make some kind of deal. He walks to the other side of the yard, the right side. There's a big round white raised stage made out of concrete. Where he imagined his plays when he was young. He told me about it on the plane. On top of it there's a small statue of the head of Martí. The liberator of Cuba. He told me he used to pray to it. He goes up to the statue and does the sign of the cross. The woman follows him, she seems moved. They shake hands again. She leaves him alone. He is sitting there. His eyes are darting back and forth. Should I do a close-up of the eyes or is that too personal? Why not. He looks like he is trying to take it all in. Take it all in. Take it all back. Breathe. That's good, Papi. He takes a cigar, he bites off the tip. Your cigar cutter is in your left pocket. Pan back and let the camera see what he is seeing. A once grand house in ruin. But still there. A child playing in the rose garden in the past. He points to the upstairs room. The room he's always been afraid of. The room where he was conceived. So he said . . . his mother told him. Do a close-up. He's smiling at me. He does love me. I'm not a stranger. I make love to you with my camera. I'm smiling back, we are together. And you are on your stage. Where you should have always been. You're back there. In your childhood. I hope you find what you are looking for. So I find what I'm looking for. My innocence. He's walking back. Pan back. Ernesto tells him he's going somewhere. He gestures fine. He gives the woman two dollars for the baby. He says . . . He's walking towards me.

FEDERICO: Turn off the camera.

(Fred turns off the camera. Federico walks in.)

FRED: So . . .

FEDERICO: She wouldn't let me in.

FRED: I know.

FEDERICO: She said to come back on Monday when the principal is there.

FRED: Who is she?

FEDERICO: The janitor. Bitch.

FRED: What?

FEDERICO: She had the keys in her hands.

FRED: Bitch. But we'll come back on Monday.

FEDERICO: Maybe. I don't know.

FRED: It hurt you.

FEDERICO: You filmed it; you tell me.

FRED: Yes. Monday they'll let you in.

FEDERICO: I don't care.

FRED: Okay.

FEDERICO: I don't.

FRED: Fine.

FEDERICO: Give me a Valium.

FRED: You sure?

FEDERICO: That's why we brought them.

FRED: Why?

FEDERICO: So I don't have to reveal my anger in front of Ernesto.

FRED: Okay.

(Fred starts to take out Valiums.)

Where is he?

FEDERICO: He ran into a friend.

FRED: A spy.

FEDERICO: Who cares.

FRED: Where next?

FEDERICO: Lunch.

FRED: La Terraza.

FEDERICO: Yes, the restaurant my father used to take me to. It's now a tourist trap.

You get good footage?

FRED: Yes.

FEDERICO: I'm glad.

(Ernesto enters with a large black-and-white poster of a little boy (Elian Gonzalez). He shows them the poster.)

Who is he?

ERNESTO: You haven't heard.

FEDERICO: No.

ERNESTO: Well.

FRED: Tell us.

ERNESTO: Well.

FEDERICO: Come on.

ERNESTO: I hope it doesn't insult you or your friend.

FRED: Why?

ERNESTO: You're Americans.

FEDERICO: I am not!

FRED: Come on . . .

ERNESTO: You look like one.

FEDERICO: *Pero no soy* . . .

ERNESTO: *Pareces.*

FEDERICO: *¡Vete al carajo!*

ERNESTO: *¡Qué coño!*

FRED: Fight in English.

FEDERICO: We are not fighting.

ERNESTO: Debating.

FRED: Right.

FEDERICO: So tell us your story. Insult us.

FRED: We'll enjoy it.

FEDERICO: Absolutely.

ERNESTO: Okay.

FEDERICO: Now you sound American.

ERNESTO: Funny.

FRED: Who is this kid in the poster?

ERNESTO: A mother took a little boy in a raft. A raft that you had to pay five thousand a person to get on. So you had to be a capitalist already to go on it.

FRED: Right.

ERNESTO: Work in the tourist trade or be a whore.

FEDERICO: Both of which corrupt?

ERNESTO: Yes.

FEDERICO: I agree.

FRED: So we are corrupting you.

ERNESTO: Yes.

FEDERICO: The story.

ERNESTO: Everyone drowned but the little boy.

FRED: Where is he?

ERNESTO: In Miami.

FEDERICO: Poor boy.

ERNESTO: With his cousins.

FEDERICO: Doomed.

ERNESTO: The father is here. His grandparents. On both sides.

FEDERICO: And they want him back?

ERNESTO: Of course.

FEDERICO: When they let me go, you weren't that interested in getting me back.

ERNESTO: We will never let Peter Pan happen again. Tragedy and shame.

FEDERICO: Shambles.

FRED: Why the rally?

ERNESTO: Because we are going to demand that he come back. Home.

FEDERICO: In the period of "family reconciliation."

ERNESTO: Yes.

FEDERICO: In the middle of this civil war that we live in?

ERNESTO: Revolution.

FEDERICO: Tinged with civil war. How many relatives do you have in Miami?

ERNESTO: Many.

FEDERICO: Which one hurt you when they left.

ERNESTO: She . . .

FRED: She.

ERNESTO: She left. My sister. They won't keep him.

FEDERICO: Who?

ERNESTO: Elian. The imperialist and that Cuban Mafia have him.

FEDERICO: I see . . .

FRED: Where to next?

ERNESTO: Right.

FRED: La Terraza.

FEDERICO: No, the rally.

ERNESTO: Are you sure?

FEDERICO: If I am from here. I want to know what here is like.

(Ernesto hands Fred the poster.)

FRED: If I put this in my suitcase, will they know I went to Cuba?

FEDERICO: Yes.

ERNESTO: It's not a souvenir.

FRED: Of course not.

ERNESTO: They're going to yell nasty things about you Cubans in Miami.

FEDERICO: I'm not from Miami.

ERNESTO: You won't be insulted.

FEDERICO: I wish someone would have fought to get me back.

ERNESTO: Instead we let you go.

FEDERICO: Yes, and thirteen thousand more just like me.

ERNESTO: I am sorry.

FEDERICO: Yes.

ERNESTO: Welcome home.

FRED: Where is it?

ERNESTO: Down the hill.

FRED: Let's walk down the hill.

ERNESTO: We won't let it happen again.

FRED: Look at that crowd.

ERNESTO: And in an hour they'll go to La Habana, to El Malecón. People from the entire island.

FRED: So this is the pre-rally.

ERNESTO: The rehearsal, yes.

FRED: I'm excited.

ERNESTO: Yes.

(Ernesto leaves.)

FEDERICO: Let's take another taxi and get the fuck out of here.

FRED: No.

FEDERICO: I'm getting out of here.

FRED: Why.

FEDERICO: You don't know!

FRED: No, this is really seeing the people. I want to be with the people.

FEDERICO: Bunch of commies. That's what's down there. Block committee members.

FRED: What? I thought you believed in Marx.

FEDERICO: But Fidel is a Leninist, maybe even a Stalinist, that has nothing to do with Marx.

FRED: It's gonna be exciting.

FEDERICO: What if there's a camera, CNN down there. And the government back there in the good old U.S. of A. sees we are here and fine us fifty thousand dollars. Or ten years in jail. That's right.

FRED: I didn't think of that.

FEDERICO: Well think about it.

FRED: Let's not go.

FEDERICO: Okay.

FRED: A cab to La Terraza.

FEDERICO: Good.

FRED: You got it.

FEDERICO: Fuck that. Let them fine me, motherfuckers. I have the right to be here. First amendment and all that crap. I want to go to jail! I want to go to jail for my country.

FRED: Okay.

FEDERICO: Yeah.

FRED: Yeah. The cameras will be at the real rally anyway. Let's go.

FEDERICO: Yes!

FRED: All right, move.

FEDERICO: My grandfather . . .

FRED: Yes?

FEDERICO: They took over his bank account and gave him two hundred dollars a person per household. That's what they turned a lifetime's savings into. Two hundred dollars a person. Then they nationalized the busses.

FRED: They?

FEDERICO: Fidel and Ché.

FRED: Do you want to go or not?

FEDERICO: Walk down the hill or not?

FRED: Yeah.

FEDERICO: After you walk down there's no going back.

FRED: Maybe there is.

FEDERICO: Turn completely away from what my parents taught me.

FRED: Okay, let's go have lunch.

FEDERICO: Fuck my grandfather and his money. I want to be here. Fidel was right.

FRED: Good! Let's go. Come on. Move! Wait, I need a new tape.

FEDERICO: In high school. I had a girlfriend who made me burn the American flag, for the cameras.

FRED: During the Vietnam war?

FEDERICO: She told me if I loved her I'd set it on fire. Let's go.

FRED: Wait. Wait for me.

FEDERICO: Yes. NBC was there so I burned the flag. It made me feel guilty and excited. My parents were horrified. "We didn't take you away from Communism so you could become a Communist."

FRED: They said that?

FEDERICO: Yes.

FRED: I'm ready. Put on the hats we bought. The sun is scorching.

FEDERICO: Yes, I think we should wear them.

(Fred takes two straw hats, he places one on Federico's head and the other on his own. They walk down stage.)

FRED: Look at him, he's already down there with his poster. I wish we had a poster.

GIRL'S VOICE: *Feliz cumpleaños Elian . . .*

(The crowd goes wild.)

FEDERICO: Who's speaking?

FRED: Let me find her with my lens. A young girl . . . maybe eighteen. She's very pregnant.

FEDERICO: Film her.

FRED: I am. She's dramatic like an actress.

FEDERICO: Except she means it.

FRED: So do actors.

FEDERICO: She means it for real.

(They walk toward the voice. To the tip of the stage. Ernesto runs toward them. He has two other posters.)

GIRL'S VOICE: *Porque queremos que esté aquí con nosotros.*
CROWD'S VOICE: *¡Sí! ¡Elian sí!*
FRED: They are going wild.
ERNESTO: Here are posters, everybody has to have one. And put your camera away.
FRED: Fuck!
ERNESTO: See you down there.
FRED: I'm going to put it in my hat and leave it running. At least we'll have audio.
FEDERICO: Poke a hole in the hat.

(They poke a small hole in the hat. Fred wears it; the camera lens sticks out.)

FRED: Can't see it?
FEDERICO: Only if I was looking for it.
FRED: See, I told you.
FEDERICO: What?
FRED: That we needed the hats.
GIRL'S VOICE: *¡Elian, te queremos!*
FRED: *Sí.* I look like a Cuban, don't I?

(He lifts up the poster.)

FEDERICO: You do.
FRED: Hold up your banner.
FEDERICO: I feel guilty and exited.
FRED: Really?
FEDERICO: I'm not here on vacation.
FRED: Neither am I.
GIRL'S VOICE: *Porque el niño que yo tengo aquí en mi vientre nunca se lo daría a los imperialistas. Este niño va a vivir . . .*
FRED: Translate.

FEDERICO: Because this child that I have inside my uterus. I would never give to the imperialist. Because this child is going to live . . .

GIRL'S VOICE: *Conmigo aquí. En Cuba. Porque él es Cubano.*

FEDERICO: Is going to live with me. Here in Cuba, because he is Cuban.

GIRL'S VOICE: *Que devuelvan a Elian.*

CROWD'S VOICE: *Que devuelvan a Elian.*

FEDERICO: Return Elian!

GIRL'S VOICE: *¡Porque este niño no es mio! ¡Ni de su padre! ¡El es hijo de Fidel!*

FEDERICO: Because he is not my child! Or his father's child! He is Fidel's child!

FRED: That's scary.

FEDERICO: But true.

(Federico lifts up his poster.)

FRED: How does it feel?

FEDERICO: Guilty and free. Return Elian! Motherfuckers.

FRED: I wish I could take a picture.

FEDERICO: Take it.

FRED: They'll get angry.

ERNESTO: Take it.

FEDERICO: I don't care who gets angry!

(Lights switch.)

> Red.
> Fire.
> Flag.
> I'm on fire.
> Pour rum all over me.
> Light the match
> and I'll be free.
> Ah.
> I'm home.

Red.
Fire.
Elian come back.
Red.
Blood.
Fire.
All over me.
Red.
Not alone.
Home.

(The crowd is chanting "Return Elian" in Spanish ("Que devuelvan a Elian.") Fred takes the camera and photographs Federico.)

FRED: Great shot.
FEDERICO: Return Elian.
ALL: *Que devuelvan a Elian.*

(Blackout.)

ACT TWO

SCENE 1

The stage. Cuba. Noon. Fred is filming. Ernesto walks in.

ERNESTO: He's not out?

FRED: He's not in, how can he be out? She didn't let him in again.

ERNESTO: I meant out of the yard.

FRED: They're arguing. That's what happens, when two ideologies clash.

ERNESTO: His temper will get him nowhere. That's part of being from the ruling class.

FRED: I know.

ERNESTO: What an attitude your friend has. He acts superior. She can smell it, she will not budge. Believe me.

FRED: Yeah.

ERNESTO: I have the pictures ready for you.

FRED: Good.

ERNESTO: Don't you want to see them?

FRED: In a minute.

(Ernesto takes pictures out of a manila envelope.)

ERNESTO: Special ... beautiful ... taken with your digital camera. Of
my sculpting ... at sunrise. The light hit it like ...

FRED: I'm sure.

ERNESTO: Take a look.

FRED: In a minute.

ERNESTO: You've got to watch his every move.

FRED: You need some money?

ERNESTO: No. Really, no ... well ... how much?

FRED: How much do you need?

ERNESTO: I want to earn it.

FRED: You have, putting up with him. Here's forty. Now let me
film.

(Ernesto takes money.)

Good.

ERNESTO: How do you do it?

FRED: What?

ERNESTO: He's in love with you, isn't he?

FRED: No! You think so?

ERNESTO: He's always grabbing your arms, your legs.

FRED: You Cubans are very touchy.

ERNESTO: I've never touched you.

FRED: True.

ERNESTO: And I would never—

FRED: He's needy.

ERNESTO: We all need.

FRED: Yes. You need dollars, he needs—

ERNESTO: Your body?

FRED: No. My body? Maybe. No. Believe me, he falls in love with
sadists. Believe me. I am too nice a guy for him.

ERNESTO: I try.

FRED: What?

ERNESTO: To understand people like you.

FRED: Americans?

ERNESTO: Sure, Americans.

FRED: Good. I understand your goals and ideals. And I will work to stop the embargo, for the rest of my life!

ERNESTO: Good. Sure you will . . . thank you.

(Fred points his camera.)

FRED: So go talk to the lady.

ERNESTO: The principal?

FRED: Yes. See if you can do something. He needs to get inside the house. For the journey to be complete.

ERNESTO: You bring him over here first.

FRED: But . . .

ERNESTO: Please.

FRED: Sure.

(Fred hands Ernesto the camera. Ernesto turns it on himself.)

ERNESTO: I never thought I'd break the rules. The rules of Marxism. Catering to the frivolity of the bourgeoisie. The hard-on over a dollar. The lure of capital. Fred, edit this out tonight please. As ever your comrade, Ernesto.

(Ernesto turns off the camera. Federico enters; Fred follows.)

FEDERICO: Okay.

ERNESTO: Okay?

FEDERICO: Talk some sense into her now.

FRED: Relax, baby. Papi.

FEDERICO: You don't know.

ERNESTO: Okay. I'll be right back.

(Ernesto exits.)

FRED: I'm here. Fred is here. Everything is under control.

FEDERICO: Yeah?

FRED: I am in charge of this trip.

FEDERICO: Why do I care. There are only bad memories waiting for me in there.

FRED: It will work out.

FEDERICO: I don't think so.

FRED: You're upset.

FEDERICO: We should have gone to the beach.

FRED: We'll go to Varadero tomorrow.

FEDERICO: Why did they say that they would let me in on Monday?

FRED: I don't know.

FEDERICO: They want to fuck with me. That's why.

FRED: Maybe.

FEDERICO: They won't forgive us for leaving.

FRED: You might be right.

FEDERICO: They're so fucking self-righteous 'cause they stayed.

FRED: Calm down.

FEDERICO: Where are the pills?

FRED: Well . . .

FEDERICO: What?

FRED: I left them back in our room.

FEDERICO: And I'm supposed to trust you.

FRED: Sorry.

FEDERICO: Fuckers.

FRED: Take a deep breath.

FEDERICO: Take a deep breath?

FRED: Okay.

(Fred takes a deep breath.)

FEDERICO: I was asking you a question.

FRED: Okay.

FEDERICO: Not telling you to do it.

FRED: Okay.

FEDERICO: Stop agreeing with me.

FRED: Will you just fucking try to breathe!

(Federico tries to breathe.)

FEDERICO: Fucking bitch. I'm so fucking angry! Fucking country!

FRED: She's just a bureaucrat. She doesn't represent the revolution.

FEDERICO: The revolution?

FRED: Yes.

FEDERICO: What the fuck do you know about the revolution!

FRED: I've learned. Since I've been here. I've learned a thing or two!

FEDERICO: The bullshit that Ernesto talks about all day long. That guy contradicts himself. Every five minutes.

FRED: Just like you.

FEDERICO: You think I contradict myself.

FRED: Yes. Come on. One breath is better then a Valium.

FEDERICO: If I breathe. I'll scream.

FRED: That's okay.

(Federico tries to breathe.)

FEDERICO: Oh God!

FRED: Yes?

FEDERICO: Fuck!

FRED: Good.

FEDERICO: Yeah!

FRED: Yeah. That's it, let it out.

FEDERICO: I don't want to start to shake.

FRED: You won't.

(Federico breathes.)

FEDERICO: Vomit. Assholes on both sides. A race full of fucking assholes. I hate my fucking father! And fucking Jorge Mascanosa, I don't care if he's dead! And the whole Cuban National Foundation. And Clinton and Jesse Helms! I hate fucking Fidel! And his brother Raul! But most of all I hate that fucking bitch that won't let me inside my house!

FRED: Feel better?

FEDERICO: Yes.

FRED: Good.

FEDERICO: Are you becoming a revolutionary, Fred?

FRED: Yes.

FEDERICO: Why?

FRED: Because I know they're right.

FEDERICO: How do you know that?

FRED: Because I'm privileged.

FEDERICO: Because you are rich?

FRED: Not rich, well off.

FEDERICO: Admit it, rich.

FRED: All right . . . rich. And I know people like my father run the world. And they're not generous. Believe me.

FEDERICO: And you feel guilty.

FRED: For the time being. Yes.

FEDERICO: So do I.

FRED: You do?

FEDERICO: I never felt so much what class I come from. This country makes you feel that. All the time. I hate myself.

FRED: Don't.

FEDERICO: Bourgeoisie through and through. That's you and me.

FRED: That we recognize it. That's the first step.

FEDERICO: I always recognized it. But now I feel it. I hate myself.

FRED: I hate myself.

FEDERICO: My petty concerns.

FRED: Mine.

FEDERICO: Got to get through it.

FRED: You'll become a proletariat yet.

FEDERICO: What's taking him so long?

FRED: Ernesto is trying to talk the principal into it. I gave him forty bucks.

FEDERICO: You gotta stop giving him such big tips.

FRED: It's nothing to me and a month's worth of food for him.

FEDERICO: You gotta be careful how you treat the help.

FRED: The help? Federico, Ernesto is our friend.

FEDERICO: He might be your friend but he's my driver.

FRED: You don't mean that.

(Fred takes out his camera, focuses it.)

Now I'm the spy.

FEDERICO: They know what you're doing.

FRED: So what.

FEDERICO: A spy is someone who goes undetected.

FRED: He's saying, "Why not. Please, come on." She shakes her head no. She points at some children. She's tough. But he hasn't given up. Keep going comrade.

(Ernesto runs in.)

FEDERICO: Am I walking in now to the house?

ERNESTO: She needs to make a call. The Writers' Union ... They're sponsoring you, right? Lizette Villa? If Lizette Villa says you can get in, you can get in.

FRED: Lizette loves him.

ERNESTO: Then no problem.

FEDERICO: Maybe we should give Lizette the forty.

ERNESTO: What?

FEDERICO: My friend and I tip generously.

ERNESTO: Well you got to go and come back a big man. Charmed life.

FEDERICO: That doesn't take into account the thirty-eight years in between.

ERNESTO: Abandoned your country, then come back and hand out dollars.

FEDERICO: I didn't decide to leave here. It was not my decision ...

FRED: Any more than Elian.

FEDERICO: I was sent away. I was, my childhood was stolen. Is that self-pity?

ERNESTO: Maybe.

FRED: No.

FEDERICO: I was totally dependent on her, my mother, and she betrayed me.

ERNESTO: We've all been betrayed.

FEDERICO: I feel like a woman who flies up to the sky and then falls into the ocean. Every time I stand in front of this fucking house. I feel like a woman. Who wants her husband back no matter if the price is her pride.

ERNESTO: I'll go see if Lizette's called.

FEDERICO: Give the principal some money.

ERNESTO: No.

FEDERICO: I'll talk to her.

ERNESTO: No. No. You get too emotional. It won't do any good.

FEDERICO: Emotion?

ERNESTO: Yes.

FRED: Why?

ERNESTO: Because in Marxism. Logic is God.

FRED: Oh.

ERNESTO: You see.

FRED: Yes.

ERNESTO: And if he tells her he feels like a woman. We are in trouble.

FEDERICO: Jesus! Dollars are God here! Who the fuck are we kidding. Here take . . .

ERNESTO: No, this one is a real communist, she won't take money.

FEDERICO: Not like you.

ERNESTO: No. An Italian restaurant has corrupted me. I own a car. Tourists pay me to drive them around.

(Ernesto exits.)

FEDERICO: Son of a bitch called me a tourist.

FRED: You feel like a woman?

FEDERICO: What?

FRED: You said that you feel like a woman. You said she flew, then fell. No pride . . .

FEDERICO: Yes, so what!

FRED: I feel like a woman. I'm not gay, but I feel like a woman.

FEDERICO: Two girls lost in La Habana?

FRED: What?

FEDERICO: You and I. Two girls lost in La Habana. *(Imitates Blanche)* Did you take a car down El Malecón, through a tunnel, to a town called Cojímar . . .

FRED: Stop it!

FEDERICO: Come on, do Blanche for me. Are you Blanche inside that macho body? Does Blanche really dwell inside your soul?

FRED: Stop it! Don't make fun of me.

(Fred sulks.)

FEDERICO: Jesus, Fred?

FRED: I tell you something about myself . . .

FEDERICO: Oh.

FRED: Something fragile inside of me and you exploit it.

FEDERICO: Sorry, I don't like it when you talk that bullshit.

FRED: "Talk that bullshit"! My insides are bullshit to you!

FEDERICO: No . . . But that girl stuff . . . when you finger a dress, or put on a little lipstick . . . And that time you went through Natasha's closet and tried on her dresses and modeled.

FRED: Let me tell you something! I fucked Natasha good and hard that night. Yeah! Good and hard!

FEDERICO: Really?

FRED: Yeah, gave it to her. Gave it . . .

FEDERICO: I believe you.

FRED: All night long, baby. I left her begging for more. Yeah.

FEDERICO: Please stop talking like that!

FRED: Like what?

FEDERICO: Like a '50s man.

FRED: '50s man and '90s chick. What a combination. What the fuck? Jesus, what a mess.

(Fred starts to cry.)

FEDERICO: Fred, don't. Don't you dare fall apart on me.

FRED: I once looked in the mirror at my face and I saw a line going up and down, dividing my face . . . the line went all the way down my body, one side masculine, the other feminine. I could not move for hours, it was all too clear, I felt so weak. Divided, I don't know where to run. Split. And it scares the shit out of me. Hold me!

FEDERICO: Hold you?

FRED: Yes. Hold me.

FEDERICO: Hold you?

FRED: Yes, please!

FEDERICO: Well . . . no . . . I don't want to hold you. I don't want to hold a man on the block where I come from. Not here.

FRED: Look beyond my manly body. See the girl that needs you.

(Fred cries.)

FEDERICO: I'm frozen.

FRED: Please.

FEDERICO: I'm angry!

FRED: 'Cause I need you?

FEDERICO: 'Cause you'll use me.

FRED: No, that I need you!

FEDERICO: That you'll ask me to open up every part of me. My heart, my brain, my nipples, my thighs, my testicles, my penis . . . And then you'll tell me . . . "What do you think I am?"

FRED: You know I'm straight.

FEDERICO: You are not at this moment.

FRED: What?

FEDERICO: You are not straight at this moment.

FRED: No. At this moment . . . I need a man . . . I need you. Please. Look at me, I'm not hiding anything.

FEDERICO: No, you're not.

FRED: No. This is me.

FEDERICO: I . . . am . . . walking toward you . . .

(They embrace. They touch each other. They kiss each other's necks. They look into each other's eyes.)

FRED: We just held each other.

FEDERICO: I know.

FRED: Yes.

FEDERICO: Yes.

FRED: Don't stop.

FEDERICO: All right.

FRED: We are holding each other.

FEDERICO: Like lovers.

FRED: I kissed your neck.

FEDERICO: I kissed yours.

(They kiss each other's necks again.)

You grabbed my ass.

FRED: Yeah.

FEDERICO: We are looking into each other's eyes.

FRED: Take me in.

FEDERICO: If I take you in . . . if I take you in . . . we'd be lovers.

FRED: Maybe. Maybe not.

FEDERICO: No.

(Federico closes his eyes.)

FRED: Open them. Open your eyes!

FEDERICO: I can't.

FRED: In them I feel whole. Thank you.

FEDERICO: Sure.

FRED: See everything?

FEDERICO: Yes.

FRED: Good.

FEDERICO: I love you.

FRED: And . . . I love you.

FEDERICO: Really?

(Federico opens his eyes.)

FRED: You are a very needy person. So am I.

FEDERICO: Yes.

FRED: My friend.
FEDERICO: What?
FRED: Come back.

(Fred kisses Federico on the mouth. Federico pulls away.)

FEDERICO: My mouth opened.
FRED: I can forgive you.
FEDERICO: My bambino. My beautiful bambino.
FRED: My grandfather—
FEDERICO: Used to call you that.
FRED: Yes.

(Fred buries his face on Federico's chest.)

FEDERICO: If I had milk I'd suckle you.
FRED: You are suckling me.
FEDERICO: What a mess.
FRED: I'm not some nice stranger.
FEDERICO: You never were.

(They hold each other.)

FRED: Is anybody looking at us?
FEDERICO: Someone is always looking at us.
FRED: Who gives a fuck.
FEDERICO *(Sings)*: "Hey there Georgy girl. There's another Georgy deep inside."
FRED *(Sings)*: "Me and my shadow all alone and feeling blue."
FEDERICO: "And when it's twelve o'clock. I climb the stairs . . ."

(They dance.)

FRED: "We never knock . . ."
FRED AND FEDERICO: "'Cause nobody's there, just me and my shadow all alone."

FRED: Not alone.

FEDERICO: And feeling fine.

FRED: I want to be a man. But not a stereotype like my dad. "Where are the broads. She's got great tits but she's a little bottom-heavy. Want to get it in. You're getting too emotional, honey. You gotta cut me loose." I hate it when I say shit like that. I sound just like him.

FEDERICO: Yes.

FRED: A man who can love a woman like a woman. That's what I want to be. That's what this country is bringing out in me.

FEDERICO: That's every girl's dream.

FRED: You think?

FEDERICO: Oh yes. Let's get out of here. Go get Ernesto. I've been inside of you. Emotionally, I mean.

FRED: You can get inside my emotions whenever you want.

FEDERICO: And inside of you, Fred, it's very warm and reassuring. I don't need to see the inside of that fucking house! Get him!

(Ernesto enters.)

FRED: It's like you can read our thoughts.

ERNESTO: Maybe your camera is bugged.

FRED: I knew it!

ERNESTO: It was a joke.

FRED: Really?

ERNESTO: I'm an artist. I don't work for the state.

FEDERICO: But you believe in the state.

ERNESTO: That's different than working for it.

FRED: Is it?

ERNESTO: One is corrupt. The other is not.

FRED: Maybe you have a point.

FEDERICO: So?

ERNESTO: Not today. Lizette is shooting a documentary in Santiago. Couldn't get her on the phone.

FEDERICO: Not today. *Mañana.*

FRED: The story of bureaucrats.

ERNESTO: But there is the rally. Look, they're in color.

FRED: It would look less organized . . . if people had different designs.

ERNESTO: Really.

FRED: It might look like this is all organized by the government. Maybe we've had enough of rallies.

ERNESTO: What.

FEDERICO: Maybe the mother did want him in Miami.

ERNESTO: The mother did. But we don't.

FEDERICO: Maybe you don't have the right. To decide. She died. You didn't.

ERNESTO: Just 'cause you don't get your way, you turn on us.

FEDERICO: You got a double standard. You know that?

ERNESTO: No. Tell me what you mean by that.

FEDERICO: I should try to help you get the boy back. But you don't even try to let me have a peek inside my house. My house. My house.

ERNESTO: You're just like the rest. Give me, give me. Give me.

FEDERICO: Well, I'm a tourist, aren't I?

ERNESTO: What?

FEDERICO: You're the one that called us tourists.

ERNESTO: Just like my sister, spoiled.

FEDERICO: Worms.

FRED: What?

FEDERICO: That's what they called us. When we left. Worms that were rotting the apple. Let the worms go. Now we're butterflies. Butterflies with dollars for wings.

ERNESTO: It's not just the dollars.

FEDERICO: No?

ERNESTO: In the period of "family reconciliation." You think it's easy for us here waiting.

FRED: Waiting?

ERNESTO: For all of you to return.

FEDERICO: Waiting for us to return. That's a little hypocritical.

ERNESTO: I am not a hypocrite. You think you're the only one that suffered. Little boy alone in the big mean U.S.A. Little boy lost. That's an easy one.

FEDERICO: You know so much. Do you know what it's like to be called a Spic? That's what we are in the U.S.A., Spics.

ERNESTO: My sister is a Spic there?

FRED: And I'm a Wop. We are Spics and Wops. So let's be friends.

FEDERICO: Your sister was called every name in the book. She worked in a factory, she became a second class citizen. Did you ask her how rough her life has been. Or did you just ask her for handouts?

ERNESTO: I haven't spoken to my sister in nineteen years. When I'm with you I think of her. I miss her and I hate her. I think of the letter that I will write, that you will take to her. If I have the courage.

FEDERICO: Are you going to ask for forgiveness?

ERNESTO: Forgive what?

FEDERICO: Being a commie.

ERNESTO: I'm proud of that. I had the courage to stay!

FEDERICO: Up yours!

FRED: Wait! Can't you hear the sea?

FEDERICO: What?

FRED: Listen to the sea. You can hear the sea from your house.

ERNESTO: No, not his house. The house. Not his country. My country. I stayed! I own it!

FEDERICO: You stole it!

ERNESTO: You abandoned it!

FRED: I think I can hear your sister calling you.

ERNESTO: Fuck off, you fag!

FRED: Who you calling a fag?

ERNESTO: You.

FRED: Well . . . gay is the proper term.

ERNESTO: In this country a fag is a fag. Not happy.

FEDERICO: And a bigot to boot.

ERNESTO: You fags! I should say. You limp-wristed . . .

FEDERICO: We don't fuck.

ERNESTO: Fags that don't fuck, what's the point.

FEDERICO: What are you?

ERNESTO: I'm a man!

FEDERICO: A puppet. Begging for a dime. Kissing Italian and Spanish ass. For a dime.

ERNESTO: Survival.

FEDERICO: I've never kissed ass.

ERNESTO: No, you were too busy on your knees.

FRED: I'm not kidding, I hear her voice in the sea.

ERNESTO: What is she saying? Leave me alone. Don't speak to me. There's a wall between us that is a hundred thousand feet high, it has embargo written on it. Don't cross it.

FEDERICO: I crossed it, already.

FRED: Listen please.

ERNESTO: I haven't spoken to my sister in nineteen years. The first five years, she made the calls once a month. The letters filled with pity, the gum inside. The razor blades so I could shave at fifteen . . . so I wouldn't look like Fidel. The assumptions.

(Drums play.)

FRED: Listen. Please. Listen. "Loneliness no matter how many cars. Loneliness. Ice is falling from the sky. Alone, calling out to you. When I eat ham, is he eating ham?"

ERNESTO: No, I am not eating ham. I'm eating a drop of rice. Stop it!

FRED: "When I used soap. Have you washed? *Mi hermano. Mi único hermano.*"

ERNESTO: It's too late.

FRED: "No."

ERNESTO: Too much time apart.

FRED: "No."

ERNESTO: I want to survive here. I don't want anything from the imperialist or the Miami Mafia.

FEDERICO: Your prized possession is an American car.

(The drums stop. Fred is out of breath.)

FRED: I can't hear the sea anymore. She's gone. You guys ruined it.

ERNESTO: Yes, an American car that does not exist in the U.S. anymore. That we struggled for forty years to keep running.

FEDERICO: You have. So what!

ERNESTO: That we valued. That we did not throw away.

FEDERICO: I haven't thrown away anything.

ERNESTO: Except who you are.

FEDERICO: Go to hell!

ERNESTO: Look at you. You're here with a friend that you don't even make love to. Instead of a wife, or a mother, or at least a male lover. You hold onto him and he's not even aware of your desperation.

FEDERICO: My desperation. What desperation?

ERNESTO: To be something. To take care of someone. Even a stranger.

FRED: I am not a stranger.

ERNESTO: In the period of "family reconciliation," I have to try to make peace with you . . . anyone that reminds me of my sister. No mater how loathsome I find them to be.

FRED: Because she will not make peace with you.

ERNESTO: No, she won't.

FEDERICO: I see why.

FRED: She tried.

ERNESTO: In your imagination.

FRED: No.

ERNESTO: Too many mojitos.

FRED: It was real.

ERNESTO: Cuban rum can be deadly, believe me.

FRED: I'm sure I heard her in the waves. And then you started fighting and ruined it all.

ERNESTO: All you heard was the ocean hitting the sand.

FEDERICO: Fred, tomorrow we are renting a car.

FRED: He doesn't mean that.

FEDERICO: I won't pay somebody that thinks I'm loathsome.

ERNESTO: My sister stopped speaking to me nineteen years ago . . . because I refused to get on the boat she had sent for me to the port of Mariel.

FEDERICO: You betrayed her. I see.

ERNESTO: I didn't ask her for the boat. I didn't ask to leave . . . and the fucking thing is that I still love her.

FRED: At least you two know what it is you're arguing about.

FEDERICO: And what is that?

FRED: The beauty of this land.

(Fred takes a poster and walks away.)

FEDERICO: We ruined it for him.

ERNESTO: Yes. He's a mystical Marxist.

FEDERICO: A clairvoyant comrade. He wants everything fast.

ERNESTO: He wants to think there's one right way. Make up. Compromise. No regret. Everybody from over there is like that.

FEDERICO: Over where?

ERNESTO: The U.S.A.

FEDERICO: Actually, I am not like that. Actually, I try to look at both sides.

ERNESTO: What if there are twenty-two sides?

FEDERICO: Then, that is chaos.

ERNESTO: Then that is what—

FEDERICO: What this is?

ERNESTO: No, what your soul is.

FEDERICO: No, you don't. Don't start again.

ERNESTO: Do you know the real meaning of not having a place in the world? A window that's never opened. Of being walled out. Of being that forbidden, exotic, sexy place . . . In the middle of the sea. Pandora's box. Demonized and tortured. But by you. By people like you.

FEDERICO: Peter Pan. Peter Pan. Tinker Bell. I believe. I believe in fairies. I believe in communists. I believe you. I believe you suffered. I believe we wanted to strangle the life out of you.

ERNESTO: You do?

FEDERICO: I believe your living in isolation was worse than my living isolated from you. Ernesto.

ERNESTO: You remembered my name.

FEDERICO: I will never forget it, Ernesto. Ernesto, forgive me.

ERNESTO: I am trying.

FEDERICO: I want to be your family. I want to when I leave here . . . to know that you know my name. That someone in my country is thinking of me.

ERNESTO: You don't want to hurt me anymore?

FEDERICO: I will do everything I can to end the embargo.

ERNESTO: I need proof.

FEDERICO: I mean it.

ERNESTO: Peter Pan. What an odd name. We sent thirteen thousand children away from their bicycles, their dolls, their toy guns. The parents that loved them—even though they were misguided.

(The drums begin to play.)

They used to use drums to talk to each other.

FEDERICO: To send different messages, from plantation to plantation.

ERNESTO: To announce a birth, a beating, a death.

FEDERICO: A revolution.

ERNESTO: Listen.

FEDERICO: Yes.

(They listen.)

What?

ERNESTO: They are saying the healing has begun. Federico.

(Blackout.)

SCENE 2

We hear the sound of airplanes landing and taking off. La Habana airport. Lights up on Ernesto, Federico and Fred. They are all smoking cigars.

FEDERICO: Delicious.

FRED: Yeah.

ERNESTO: The real thing.

FRED: Thanks for taking us to the factory.

ERNESTO: Sure. You know even in La Habana they'll sell you fakes.

FEDERICO: But these are not fake, I can taste a fake. When we get to Cancun we have to take off the labels.

FRED: Yep. Fucking embargo.

ERNESTO: Yeah. Maybe the cigar smokers in the U.S. will be the ones that stop the embargo.

FRED: That would be a trip. I think we should also hide them . . . in chocolate boxes.

FEDERICO: You carry them. Because there is no doubt that they are going to check my bags.

ERNESTO: Good idea.

FRED: Yeah. *(He smokes)* What a taste.

FEDERICO: I had a dream right before I woke up this morning. I was in a taxi in L.A. The taxi guy asked me where I lived and I couldn't remember. We went down one street and another but I couldn't remember where I lived. I was lost.

FRED: Did you ever get there?

FEDERICO: The only address I could remember was of a house in Hialeah. Funny. It's made me anxious.

FRED: Maybe you were anxious and that's why you had the dream.

FEDERICO: No, the dream made me anxious.

(He takes a long drag from his cigar.)

FRED: You're smoking like a guy who's anxious.

FEDERICO: No, I'm not.

FRED: Fine.

(Fred takes a long drag from his cigar.)

FEDERICO: What do you call that?

FRED: I admit it. You've made me anxious.

FEDERICO: Of course we are anxious. We are leaving for God's sake! At least this time I know that I'm leaving.

FRED: Right.

FEDERICO: The first time . . . I didn't know.

FRED: I know.

ERNESTO: Are you ready to go?

FEDERICO: I don't know.

FRED: If you're not we will get off the plane.

FEDERICO: Sometimes this seems like home, sometimes it doesn't.

ERNESTO: Sometimes you seem like family, sometimes you don't.

FRED: Sometimes I feel like an outsider.

FEDERICO: Funny.

ERNESTO: I feel the same.

(They all three smoke.)

FRED: One thing I know for sure. Last time I'll be able to smoke without some uptight, righteous, bitch non-smoker staring at me.

FEDERICO: At least we don't live in L.A.

FRED: True. But New York is being immigrated by people who should live in L.A.

ERNESTO: They're worse in L.A.?

FRED: They live in one of the most polluted cities in the world. Each of them owns, "Like, three cars." No rapid transit. But they are anti-smoking fanatics. You can't even smoke outside in L.A.

ERNESTO: No smoking anywhere?

FRED: Just breathing their air is like having three packs a day. They are in deep denial.

FEDERICO: Denial is a concept that was invented in L.A.

ERNESTO: Here they let us smoke, but they don't let us watch American television.

FEDERICO: The world's not fair.

FRED: Nope.

ERNESTO: You are right about that. I am sorry that you never did get in.

FEDERICO: I feel like I did. Why long for a building? The buildings have crumbled. The past does not exist. Does not, will not ever come back. It only lives in photo books. Kept, maintained by both sides. For either one of us to flip through on any given afternoon on either side of the blockade. Block of ice. Block of cement. Where no semen can get through.

FRED: He means life.

ERNESTO: I understood that.

FEDERICO: I came to my island. I met you. And I found what lives inside of you. I have stood in the courtyard of my school and wondered how a boy could have been anything but a writer. That walked down those hallways into that courtyard. How did my dad ever end up being an accountant?

FRED: He denied his past.

ERNESTO: He ran away.

FEDERICO: But. I came back, Cuba. I went to the church where he married my mother. Not the courtroom in L.A. where they were divorced. I have seen the sink outside my house, granite. A granite sink. Still intact after fifty years. Cuuuu Baaa!

FRED: Cuba!

ERNESTO: Cuba. We are friends?

FEDERICO: For lack of a better word.

ERNESTO: Yes.

FEDERICO: There should be something . . . another word that describes the state of human relations that lies somewhere, between lover and friend.

ERNESTO: But there isn't.

FRED: They are calling our flight.

ERNESTO: I better go.

(Federico has taken out a dictionary from his bag.)

FEDERICO: Fred, look up "friend." See if it leads us to another word.

ERNESTO: Comrade.

FEDERICO: Overused. Not emotional enough.

ERNESTO: I should go.

FEDERICO: We got a minute.

FRED: Okay, "Friendship. One attached to another by affection or esteem. One not hostile. One that is of the same nation or group. One that favors something. Paramour. A member of a group that stresses Inner Light. Rejects ostentation. They opposed war."

FEDERICO: I think the last definition is about Quakers.

ERNESTO: Quakers?

FEDERICO: An American religion.

ERNESTO: Oh.

FEDERICO: But I was wrong. Even though "friend" is used too much to mean acquaintance nowadays. In its true definition. It does define us.

FRED: Even the bit about the Quakers?

ERNESTO: Yes.

FRED: Good-bye.

ERNESTO: Come back.

FEDERICO: I'll try.

ERNESTO: Good-bye, friend.

(He goes to Fred and kisses him quickly and sweetly on the lips.)

God. I've kissed a man in the middle of La Habana airport.

FEDERICO: We won't tell your wife.

(Fred starts to cry.)

ERNESTO: Don't cry, Fred. Please.

FRED: This is very hard. Leaving this country. Thank you.

ERNESTO: For what?

FRED: Being my friend.

ERNESTO: Federico?

FEDERICO: My humble handshake for a sincere friend?

(Ernesto and Federico shake hands.)

The embargo is melting.

ERNESTO: Not really.

FEDERICO: Between us.

ERNESTO: Because of one little boy. One little boy that made us be together in protest.

FEDERICO: Yes.

(Ernesto starts to leave. Then he turns around.)

I have a letter for my sister. It has on it her maiden name. Her married name and her last address.
FEDERICO: I'll find her.

(Ernesto hands Federico an envelope.)

FRED: We promise.
ERNESTO: Ciao.

(Ernesto runs out.)

FRED: I won't.
FEDERICO: What?
FRED: Forget him; like I do everything else in my life.
FEDERICO: I won't let you.
FRED: I won't run away. From either of you. Read the letter.
FEDERICO: I can't!
FRED: Come on!
FEDERICO: It's to his sister.
FRED: He won't care. And we might not ever find her.

(Fred takes the letter from Federico's hands and opens it.)

FEDERICO: Fred!
FRED: He didn't even seal the envelope.
FEDERICO: It's wrong.
FRED: Modesty does not become you.

(Fred looks at the letter.)

Hm?
FEDERICO: Well?
FRED: Interesting.

FEDERICO: Really?

FRED: Wow!

FEDERICO: What does it say?

FRED: I can't read it. It's in Spanish.

(Federico grabs the letter.)

Translate!

FEDERICO: Okay.

(Federico reads.)

"My dearest Sister. Rosa, it has been such a long time. So many years without a word, a note, a sentence, a postcard, a hello. I know why. I know that I disappointed you . . ."

FRED: You okay?

FEDERICO: Give me a minute.

FRED: It's okay.

FEDERICO: I've cried enough.

FRED: Take your time.

(Pause.)

FEDERICO: "I know that I have disappointed you. By not believing in what you believe. By betraying everything you hold dear . . . In your eyes, I betrayed our parents. Their store. The house which I still live in. The church, but the Pope has come back. Why can't you? I have not seen what you look like in almost twenty years. Have you aged? I bet you haven't. I bet you are still . . . still the most beautiful girl in La Habana, but you are not in La Habana anymore . . . Are you? Send me a picture please at least that . . . Here is a picture of my wife and our daughters and myself. They look like you, don't they? My daughters . . . They look like you. If this man gets this letter to you it means he forgave us. All of us that wanted a revolution. If he forgave me, why can't you? I'm still here. In our house. The same telephone number. Nothing's changed in twenty years. Time is still here . . . We are here . . . It is here . . . changed. But still recognizable . . . Waiting. Waiting for you. Everything . . . including my love . . . Your brother, Ernesto."

(A long pause.)

FRED: Are you crying?

FEDERICO: Maybe.

FRED: So am I.

FEDERICO: I am going to deliver this letter.

FRED: Oh my God! We are taking off.

FEDERICO: Yes. I can hear the motors revving up.

FRED: I'm scared of flying.

FEDERICO: Think lovely thoughts.

FRED: Really?

FEDERICO: And we will fly.

FRED: Lovely thoughts?

FEDERICO: Yes. Listen. A world where cold wars are not fought over children.

FRED: Yes.

(They start to go up in the air.)

FEDERICO: Where their childhood is not stolen from them. So they can be happy and grow up.

FRED: Without being afraid of their fathers.

FEDERICO: Yes.

FRED: Where money is not the important thing.

FEDERICO: Where cultures value each other. Where ownership is not the bottom line. Free of Imperialism.

FRED: We're flying.

(They fly.)

FEDERICO: Yes.

FRED: But . . . Well . . . How?

FEDERICO: What?

FRED: How can you get something like that. People like to own things.

FEDERICO: It's something to wish for. I don't know how.

FRED: It'll never happen. Not in our life time.

(They start to slowly fall.)

I think the engine stopped. Oh God. We are going to crash into the island. I think this is it!

FEDERICO: It's all your fault.

FRED: Why?

FEDERICO: You became cynical.

FRED: Help me!

FEDERICO: Where a small little island is allowed to stand up for itself.

FRED: Yes.

FEDERICO: And be.

FRED: Be what?

FEDERICO: Itself.

FRED: Where a person can be a man, a woman, a boy, a little girl. Whatever feels right inside.

FEDERICO: Where a child can decide where he wants to live.

FRED: Where more than one ideology can exist.

FEDERICO: More than one superpower.

FRED: Where friendship is valued as much as marriage.

FEDERICO: Where love is not a fetish.

FRED: Yes.

FEDERICO: We are going up.

(They fly.)

FRED: The motor started! The motor started!

FEDERICO: We are flying.

FRED: Yeah.

FEDERICO: Flying!

FRED: Up and away!

FEDERICO: We are going home.

FRED: Home?

FEDERICO: One of two.

FRED: Look. Look at it. The sea is drowning in the sand.

(They look down on the stage.)

FEDERICO: I'll be back! *"Mi coral en la tiniebla, iré a Santiago."*

FRED: *"Iré a Santiago."*

FEDERICO: *"El mar ahogado en la arena."*

FRED: *"Iré a Santiago."* Down there.

FEDERICO: Yes. *"O Cuba! ¡O curva de suspiro y barro!"*

FRED: *"Iré a Santiago."* Where magic happens.

(They disappear. The drums play.
Silence.
The lights come uo on Ernesto. He is holding up a poster of Elian.)

ERNESTO: Miami Mafia. Yankee politicians. Exxon and United Fruit Company. Meyer Lansky and all his disciples. You've kept us apart long enough. Return us. Motherfuckers! You've kept us apart long enough. Return us. Us. Elian. Peter Pan. Give them back. Give them back to us. Motherfuckers! Let us come together. End the embargo. Please. Motherfuckers! Give them back!

END OF PLAY

KISSING FIDEL

For my siblings:
Jesus, Jeanette, Gilda and Michelle

Kissing Fidel was originally commissioned by the Public Theater (George C. Wolfe, Artistic Director) and was first produced by INTAR Theatre (Eduardo Machado, Artistic Director) at the Kirk Theater in New York City. The play opened on September 20, 2005. The production was directed by Michael John Garcés; the set design was by Mikiko Suzuki; the lighting design was by Paul Whitaker; the costume design was by Meghan Healey and the sound design was by David M. Lawson. The stage manager was Michael Alifanz. It was performed by:

OSCAR	Bryant Mason
MIRIAM	Karen Kondazian
YOLANDA	Judith Delgado
OSVALDO	Lazaro Perez
DANIEL	Javier Rivera
ISMAEL	Andrés Munar

Characters

OSCAR MARQUES, a novelist in his forties

OSVALDO MARQUES, his father, in his sixties

MIRIAM MARQUES, his aunt, Osvaldo's sister. In her early fifties

YOLANDA GARCIA, another aunt, his mother's sister. In her early fifties

DANIEL, his cousin, Miriam's son thirty

ISMAEL, his cousin from Cuba, twenty-five

Place

Miami

Time

August 23, 1994, after midnight

ACT ONE

Miami. Midnight in a waiting room in a funeral parlor. It is a Cuban funeral home, so there is a big espresso maker to make café during the wake. The room has marble floors and modern benches. It is very posh.

Daniel, a young man of thirty, is asleep on one of the benches. He is murmuring to himself. A woman, his mother Miriam, enters. Miriam is in her early fifties, exotic and sexy. She is dressed in a purple linen dress and has a rosary in her hands. She is about to make café when she hears Daniel. She sits by where he is sleeping and listens intently. She seems worried by what she hears.

DANIEL: Ah. Oh, uh. What? Oh, Tom! Tom, Tom . . . Aah, there!

(Miriam hits him.)

MIRIAM: Wake up!
DANIEL: What, Tom? Oh . . .
MIRIAM: Daniel!

(She hits him again. This time he wakes up.)

DANIEL: God! Mamá! You scared the shit out of me.

MIRIAM: Is your psychiatrist named Tom?

DANIEL: Tom!

MIRIAM: Is he?

DANIEL: Why are you asking me?

MIRIAM: You were talking in your sleep.

DANIEL: And you listened in?

MIRIAM: Of course I did.

DANIEL: How could you!

MIRIAM: I care about my children's well-being.

DANIEL: How about privacy?

MIRIAM: There's no room for privacy between a mother and a son.

DANIEL: You told your mother everything?

MIRIAM *(Crossing herself)*: Cross yourself when you talk about my mother.

(Daniel crosses himself.)

DANIEL: Well, did you?

MIRIAM: No.

DANIEL: See.

MIRIAM: But she was so old-fashioned.

DANIEL: And you are not?

MIRIAM: No ... but she was and tomorrow we will bury her.

DANIEL: And the past.

MIRIAM: What?

DANIEL: The past will go with her.

MIRIAM: No, not the past.

DANIEL: Please, let's bury the past with her.

MIRIAM: No, the past is the bullet Fidel blasted into our hearts. The past is an open wound. It's a rose that will not wither, no matter how hard we press it against the covers of a book.

DANIEL: Things change, Mamá.

MIRIAM: Not in Miami.

DANIEL: Well, in the rest of the world.

MIRIAM: Somebody is putting crazy ideas in your head. You should have never moved away from home.

DANIEL: I am thirty years old.

MIRIAM: You should only leave home when you get married.

DANIEL: Maybe I'll be a bachelor forever.

MIRIAM: What are you saying?

DANIEL: Maybe I'll never fall in love.

MIRIAM: Who said love had anything to do with marriage?

DANIEL: Mamá, you don't mean that.

MIRIAM: Who's Tom?

DANIEL: Tom is a friend!

MIRIAM: Oh.

DANIEL: From work.

MIRIAM: A casual friend?

DANIEL: Of course. He's from North Carolina, just moved here about a year ago.

MIRIAM: So why were you screaming "Aah, Oh! There, Aah! Oh, Tom? Tom! Tom! Tom!" Why?

DANIEL: What?

MIRIAM: You still talk in your sleep.

DANIEL: Really?

MIRIAM: Yes.

DANIEL: Oh, God!

MIRIAM: You could never keep a secret.

DANIEL: I bet you keep a lot of secrets.

MIRIAM: In our family that was the only way to survive.

DANIEL: Really?

MIRIAM: Who is Tom?

DANIEL: What kind of secrets?

MIRIAM: Who the hell is Tom!

DANIEL: Well . . . I . . . was probably imagining that we were sky diving together. He wants me to jump off a plane with him.

MIRIAM: Don't you dare!

DANIEL: No. Don't worry. I don't dare.

MIRIAM: So, good. That's why you were making all those guttural "Ooh's" and "Aah's"—you were dreaming.

DANIEL: That I was falling.

MIRIAM: Good.

DANIEL: Yes, from a plane.

MIRIAM: That explains it.

DANIEL: Good.

MIRIAM: You should go and sit with my mother.

DANIEL: I don't like looking at the dead.

MIRIAM: She was your grandmother, she's . . .

DANIEL: Only a corpse now.

MIRIAM: They wanted to embalm her.

DANIEL: They do that here.

MIRIAM: Where?

DANIEL: In this country.

MIRIAM: But this is Miami.

DANIEL: Still America.

MIRIAM: But this is a Cuban funeral parlor. The most expensive Cuban funeral parlor.

DANIEL: Maybe the morticians are first generation, trained here.

MIRIAM: So what? They should then be trained to do things the way their parents did. And everybody knows that Cubans do not embalm bodies. We only mourn overnight. And a body doesn't rot in twenty-four hours, especially in air-conditioning.

(Yolanda has entered. She is also in her fifties. She is wearing a navy dress. She looks tough. Still beautiful. She has blonde hair.)

YOLANDA: Of course not. No, no, no. No trouble.

MIRIAM: They want more café?

YOLANDA: Yes.

MIRIAM: What do they think this is, a café stand?

(Miriam starts to get up.)

YOLANDA: I'll do it.

MIRIAM: Thanks.

YOLANDA: Hello, Daniel.

DANIEL: How are you, Mrs. Garcia?

YOLANDA: Fine.

DANIEL: Good.

YOLANDA: Sad but fine.

DANIEL: Yes, we all are.

YOLANDA: Is he here yet?

DANIEL: I haven't seen him.

YOLANDA: I don't think I remember what he looks like . . . goddamn you, Fidel.

MIRIAM: It's not Fidel's fault that he doesn't like visiting.

YOLANDA: Yes, it is!

MIRIAM: He does not want to see us.

DANIEL: Actually, he says that you abandoned him.

YOLANDA: You talk to him? How nice. Cousins should be close . . .

DANIEL: No, I read about him.

MIRIAM: He does not talk to any of us.

YOLANDA: He calls me once every five years.

DANIEL: Really?

YOLANDA: Yes.

DANIEL: That's interesting.

MIRIAM: No, it's not!

DANIEL: I think it is.

MIRIAM: Do you think our nephew is really coming?

YOLANDA: That's what my sister told me.

MIRIAM: My brother hasn't heard from him.

YOLANDA: That doesn't mean anything; your brother hasn't heard from him in twenty years.

DANIEL: He hates him.

YOLANDA: How do you know that?

DANIEL: I read him. There's always a character that hates his father in all his . . .

MIRIAM: Why come here?

DANIEL: Maybe he needs more material.

(Daniel laughs.)

MIRIAM: He wants to come on the day that we bury her because he wants to prove to us that the only way he will see any of us is dead. Why does he hate us? We are a good family, no?

(Pause.)

YOLANDA: He doesn't hate me. I mean us.

MIRIAM: Then how could he be so cruel about us?

YOLANDA: He always had a wild imagination.

DANIEL: He's obsessed. That's why he has to write about you obsessively.

MIRIAM: You don't even know him. I mean I remember the little boy. But the man. I've only seen a couple of times.

DANIEL: I've read his novels.

YOLANDA: I would never read them. Are they any good?

DANIEL: Yes.

YOLANDA: Who would have known.

MIRIAM: Every word in them is a lie!

DANIEL: Of course, Mamá, they're fiction. Novels.

MIRIAM: I never read them and I never want to read them!

YOLANDA: Neither do I!

DANIEL: You are not in them.

YOLANDA: I am not?

DANIEL: No.

YOLANDA: Oh.

MIRIAM: But I am and people tell me it's not a pretty picture.

DANIEL: It's not you, it's fiction.

MIRIAM: But you see me in them?

DANIEL: Well . . .

MIRIAM: Tell me. The truth!

DANIEL: Yes, there's parts of the character . . . That I recognize as you . . .

MIRIAM: What part of me?

DANIEL: The sarcastic part.

MIRIAM: Son of a bitch.

YOLANDA: You don't need to be mean about my sister.

MIRIAM: Sorry.

DANIEL: You are very funny is his books, Mamá.

YOLANDA: If he's a bastard. Doesn't make her a bitch.

MIRIAM: Of course not. It was just an expression.

YOLANDA: Oscarito was so sweet when he was a little boy. My first nephew, my sister's son. So full of charm. Then those seizures started . . . He had those visions.

MIRIAM: Psychotic episodes, hallucinations.

YOLANDA: Visions! Of men with canes banging down his windows, the windows of his bedroom, these men wanting him, wanting to take him . . .

DANIEL: Delusions of grandeur right from the beginning.

MIRIAM: What?

DANIEL: Nothing, Mamá.

YOLANDA: And he would pass out. His blood pressure down to nothing.

MIRIAM: And my mother would give him a big cup of café. With three teaspoons of sugar.

DANIEL: Why?

MIRIAM: To bring up his blood pressure.

YOLANDA: Thanks for reminding me.

MIRIAM: What?

YOLANDA: The café must be ready.

(Daniel looks at the espresso machine.)

DANIEL: Not yet. Water still coming to a boil.

YOLANDA: Oh. Fine. Well . . .

MIRIAM: She always saved him, she always held him, my mother. The woman who he hasn't seen for twenty years. And now he comes to her funeral?

YOLANDA: He changed after that.

DANIEL: What?

MIRIAM: What do you care?

DANIEL: I'm fascinated by him. Yolanda, how did he change?

YOLANDA: Well . . .

DANIEL: Tell me.

YOLANDA: Miriam?

DANIEL: Please.

MIRIAM: Tell him Yolanda, tell him the whole fascinating story.

DANIEL: Good.

YOLANDA: Well, Daniel . . .

DANIEL: Yes?

YOLANDA: During the revolution, your cousin Oscar was six . . . Before the revolution he was perfect . . . but then at six . . . your cousin Oscar changed. He became very nervous . . . we sent him to a psychiatrist. He became more isolated. And we came to this country and they moved to Los Angeles. We were all separated. No more family. He called me once when he was sixteen. He told me, "Save me, Tia, I think I'm lost. I think I'm suffering . . . I think I'm going insane, mad."

DANIEL: What did you tell him?

YOLANDA: Stop thinking.

DANIEL: What did he answer?

YOLANDA: He hung up on me.

DANIEL: And he became a writer.

MIRIAM: We are already wasting too much time talking about him. If he wants to be an outcast, let him be an outcast. Just don't let him in on the day of my funeral that's all I ask.

YOLANDA: He's your brother's son.

MIRIAM: So what?

YOLANDA: He has familial rights.

MIRIAM: Not if he hasn't been around . . .

YOLANDA: I think it has to do with blood being thicker than water.

MIRIAM: No, it has to do with being around, and performing your duty as a family member.

YOLANDA: I don't know.

MIRIAM: Please, let's drop the subject.

YOLANDA: Well . . .

MIRIAM: They wanted to embalm her.

YOLANDA: You didn't let her be . . . God! Did you?

MIRIAM: Of course not. But they fought me.

YOLANDA *(To Daniel)*: The café is ready. So they fought you?

MIRIAM: Yes. Just like when I gave birth to Daniel and they wanted to circumcise him.

DANIEL: Mamá!

MIRIAM: What?

DANIEL: Please!

MIRIAM: You should be grateful that you have all your skin on your pipi. Your wife will thank me.

84

YOLANDA: It looks prettier covered. I always thought.

MIRIAM: I said to them, I want my son to have all the skin that God intended him to have. And they lectured me about infection. I told them we don't live in the desert, we don't live in Israel, haven't you heard of showers, water and soap. I swear to you doctors, when he's young I will pull his weeny back every day and clean it and when he gets older he'll know how to do it himself. Then they told me he would give his wife cancer. I laughed, told them, "If a foreskin gives you cancer, start my chemotherapy today. You Jews can be so ridiculous." Can't they?

YOLANDA: Opinionated, they can be opinionated.

MIRIAM: They think too much.

DANIEL: How did you know they were Jews?

MIRIAM: They were doctors.

DANIEL: So?

MIRIAM: We had just gotten here from Cuba, all the doctors were Jewish. Jews like to cut it off.

YOLANDA: Catholics don't cut anything off.

DANIEL: Except your spirit.

MIRIAM: What?

DANIEL: At least Jews get taught how to think. Catholics only get taught how to sin. That, followed by guilt.

MIRIAM: Everybody feels guilty.

DANIEL: Do you?

MIRIAM: Never.

DANIEL: So you are different than everybody else?

MIRIAM: Yes, I am.

DANIEL: Sometimes I think I hate you for that.

MIRIAM: You hate me?

DANIEL: Sometimes.

MIRIAM: So what, I hated my parents all the time.

DANIEL: I know.

MIRIAM: How do you know?

DANIEL: It's in his books.

MIRIAM: The worst thing that could happen to a family is a writer.

YOLANDA: Oscar is going back.

DANIEL: What?

YOLANDA: He is!

MIRIAM: What, Yolanda! What are you talking about?

YOLANDA: Back to Cuba. Oscar wants to go back and kiss Fidel. And have a picture taken. While they are kissing!

DANIEL: It will be in the *Miami Herald* for sure!

MIRIAM: What? No, he cannot do that!

YOLANDA: He is going to do it!

MIRIAM: I am not going to let him!

DANIEL: Who told you this?

MIRIAM: Yes, who told you?

YOLANDA: My sister told me that he plans to go back there and kiss Fidel. Like that bitch lawyer, that went back. Remember?

DANIEL: She had to move out of Miami.

MIRIAM: Cubans who betray us we don't keep in business.

DANIEL: We? Who's we?

MIRIAM: The real Cubans are in Miami. He'll never sell a book in this town.

YOLANDA: My sister is hysterical. That boy will end up killing his mother.

MIRIAM: Not only is our nephew a communist. He's a . . .

DANIEL: Mamá. Please.

MIRIAM: What?

DANIEL: No ugly words.

MIRIAM: Don't get liberal on me.

DANIEL: I'm a Republican and you know it, Mamá.

MIRIAM: You ever read his books?

YOLANDA: No, of course he hasn't.

DANIEL: I told you twice. I've read his books.

MIRIAM: When did you read them?

DANIEL: When I was in college.

MIRIAM: So is he a communist?

DANIEL: He's a very complicated man.

(*Osvaldo walks in. He is in his sixties and wears a grey suit.*)

MIRIAM: Talking about complicated men.

YOLANDA: The father walks in.

OSVALDO: Whose father?

DANIEL: Oscar's.

OSVALDO: Oh, him.

MIRIAM: Your son, remember?

OSVALDO: Hardly.

YOLANDA: Bastard.

OSVALDO: I know that's what your sister thinks I am.

YOLANDA: What she knows you are. How did you manage to come here without your young wife?

OSVALDO: I'm not on a leash.

YOLANDA: Really? Could have fooled me.

MIRIAM: And me.

OSVALDO: I knew you'd gang up on me eventually.

MIRIAM: Good.

OSVALDO: We make our choices . . . and if you are a real man, you stand up for what you believe in. Remember that, Daniel.

DANIEL: Yes, sir!

YOLANDA: You stood up for what you believed in? Really?

OSVALDO: Yes, I did!

YOLANDA: What, deserting your wife and children?

MIRIAM: You are lucky they love you.

OSVALDO: How do you know they love me?

MIRIAM: I've read his books.

DANIEL: I thought you hadn't!

MIRIAM: Go and stand by Mother's casket!

DANIEL: Why?

MIRIAM: One of us should be there with Father.

OSVALDO: He is still crying.

MIRIAM: He should be, he destroyed her.

YOLANDA: Killed her. With his cheating heart.

OSVALDO: She died at ninety.

YOLANDA: So?

OSVALDO: She was as heartless as he is. No one dies for love.

YOLANDA: You are heartless.

OSVALDO: I know that's what you think about me.

YOLANDA: You destroyed my sister and your brother.

DANIEL: What?

YOLANDA: Pedro. Your brother Pedro, the one that killed himself.

MIRIAM: Yolanda!

YOLANDA: Remember?

OSVALDO: I remember him.

YOLANDA: I know you try to forget him.

OSVALDO: He was my brother, not yours.

YOLANDA: I'm the one that found him.

DANIEL: How did he do it?

MIRIAM: Never mind.

DANIEL: Why don't I know anything about him?

MIRIAM: I was pregnant with you. Why repeat a sad story?

OSVALDO: True.

DANIEL: You found him?

YOLANDA: Yes.

MIRIAM: Go be with Mother, Daniel.

DANIEL: But . . .

MIRIAM: There is nothing worse then a man who is a gossip. Go!

DANIEL: Fine.

(Daniel exits.)

MIRIAM: Fight all you want now.

OSVALDO: I know you hate me because I left your sister. But I did nothing to my brother.

YOLANDA: You owe me.

OSVALDO: What do I owe you?

YOLANDA: I take care of all the ones that you destroyed.

OSVALDO: What the hell do you mean by that?

YOLANDA: I know you remember.

(Yolanda exits.)

OSVALDO: Bitch.

MIRIAM: No she's not. She took care of our brother . . . when we left . . . she stayed with him. He killed himself. Remember?

OSVALDO: I know. But all that happened decades ago.

MIRIAM: It still happened. He cut his . . .

OSVALDO: Don't say it!

MIRIAM: Throat.

OSVALDO: Dead history.

MIRIAM: What?

OSVALDO: The past is just dead history.

MIRIAM: I think about Pedro in Cuba, at least once a day.

OSVALDO: I don't.

MIRIAM: I don't believe you.

OSVALDO: Fine, don't believe me.

MIRIAM: You think you're going to get off without payment?

OSVALDO: I have.

MIRIAM: Not while I'm alive.

OSVALDO: You have no power.

MIRIAM: You forget I saw the two of you, my brothers, holding each other like . . .

OSVALDO: Shut up!

MIRIAM: Or was I dreaming?

OSVALDO: Stop it!

MIRIAM: I think it was real . . .

OSVALDO: If you keep it up I'll leave.

MIRIAM: I can still get to you.

OSVALDO: It is Mamá's funeral, let's behave.

MIRIAM: Behave?

OSVALDO: Like adults.

MIRIAM: You think you have it all under control?

OSVALDO: Yes. And you hate me for it.

MIRIAM: Really?

OSVALDO: Really. Of course.

MIRIAM: I had lunch with him . . .

OSVALDO: Who?

MIRIAM: Our other brother. The illegitimate one.

OSVALDO: The bastard?

MIRIAM: Yes.

OSVALDO: How could you?

MIRIAM: He is our half brother. We should be friendly.

OSVALDO: Never.

MIRIAM: Now that Mother is dead. Why not?

OSVALDO: 'Cause his mother ruined our mother.

MIRIAM: Just like you ruined your wife?

OSVALDO: I did not have any more children.

MIRIAM: Papá loves her.

OSVALDO: Shut up!

MIRIAM: Her name is Carmen, and Papá loves her.

OSVALDO: I remember the day she became pregnant and knocked and knocked at the door till Mamá saw her . . . How can you talk to that bastard?

MIRIAM: He was Papá's love child, emphasis on love.

OSVALDO: Lust.

MIRIAM: Love, Papá loves her more.

OSVALDO: Than Mother?

MIRIAM: Papá loves him more.

OSVALDO: Than me?

MIRIAM: Yes, than you.

OSVALDO: Papá does not love me.

MIRIAM: Probably not.

OSVALDO: Not at all?

MIRIAM: I don't think so.

(Osvaldo starts to cry.)

Good.

OSVALDO: What?

MIRIAM: You remembered Cuba, see?

OSVALDO: See what?

MIRIAM: You are not free.

OSVALDO: I'm crying over Mamá.

MIRIAM: No, you are not. Here.

(She gives him a handkerchief.)

Blow your nose.

OSVALDO: Thank you.

MIRIAM: Nothing worse than seeing a seventy-year-old man cry . . .

OSVALDO: Sixty-five.

MIRIAM: Close to seventy.

OSVALDO: And you?

MIRIAM: I'm still in my fifties. I'm still your little sister.

(Osvaldo blows his nose. We hear a car. Miriam looks out the window.)

Good.

(He hands her the handkerchief.)

You can keep it.

OSVALDO: I won't need it.

MIRIAM: I think you are going to do a lot more crying tonight.

OSVALDO: Thanks. But I won't.

(He folds the handkerchief and puts it in his pocket.)

MIRIAM: You better go in.

OSVALDO: Why?

MIRIAM: A car just drove up.

OSVALDO: So?

MIRIAM: A cab.

OSVALDO: You think it's him?

MIRIAM: I know it is.

OSVALDO: Tell him I don't want to talk to him.

MIRIAM: He is your son. You have to talk to him!

OSVALDO: No son of mine would ever write what he wrote about me. Tell him to go!

MIRIAM: He has a right to be here.

OSVALDO: Tell him not to talk to me!

MIRIAM: Don't tell me what to do.

OSVALDO: He betrayed me.

MIRIAM: All sons betray their fathers.

OSVALDO: I never did.

MIRIAM: You should have.

OSVALDO: Tell him to go back to New York!

MIRIAM: Go pray for our mother.

OSVALDO: Yes. Fine. Everything he wrote about me is a lie.

MIRIAM: I know.

(Osvaldo exits.)

Well, really Mother, it is you that should pray for us. What a mess you have made of our lives.

(Miriam opens the door.)

Come in. I saw you drive up for christ's sakes. Welcome to Shangri-la.

(Oscar enters. He is dressed in black. He is in his early forties. Miriam gives him a look.)

Well?

OSCAR: Well . . .

MIRIAM: Here you are. In black.

OSCAR: I am not in mourning for my life.

MIRIAM: What?

OSCAR: I'm in mourning for my grandmother's life. I thought you'd enjoy the literary conceit.

MIRIAM: Did you kiss Fidel yet?

OSCAR: But as usual, you want to get right to the point. Not yet.

MIRIAM: Why are you here?

OSCAR: So many questions.

MIRIAM: You look fat.

OSCAR: So do you.

MIRIAM: I do not.

OSCAR: Actually, I've lost weight.

MIRIAM: Glad I didn't see you fatter.

OSCAR: So am I.

MIRIAM: You're losing your hair.

OSCAR: Yes I am.

MIRIAM: It used to be thick.

OSCAR: Oh, I remember.

MIRIAM: Your face has wrinkles.

OSCAR: So does yours.

MIRIAM: I can still get it anytime I want.

OSCAR: So can I.

MIRIAM: Not in the gutter where you go.

OSCAR: Really? Where do you get it? At the country club?

MIRIAM: You've led a bad life.

OSCAR: So have you.

MIRIAM: I've led a pampered life. Sure. Why not?

OSCAR: Rich bitch?

MIRIAM: Artist whore.

OSCAR: I was hoping that I missed your menopause.

MIRIAM: Still in it. You should have waited another ten years to come and visit us.

OSCAR: Well . . .

MIRIAM: Go mourn.

OSCAR: I'm not ready.

MIRIAM: I thought that's what you came here to do.

OSCAR: I hate this place.

MIRIAM: I know. I've read your novels.

OSCAR: Really?

MIRIAM: I've read your interviews.

OSCAR: Good.

MIRIAM: I've been privy to the gossip.

OSCAR: Gossip?

MIRIAM: That you call your life.

OSCAR: They ask you if you're related to me. Don't they?

MIRIAM: Who?

OSCAR: People, my fans.

MIRIAM: You are a writer. People don't care very much about writers. You should have been a singer if you wanted that kind of attention.

OSCAR: They ask you. And you hate admitting it. Don't you?

MIRIAM: I don't think about you very often.

OSCAR: But they ask you?

MIRIAM: Sometimes.

OSCAR: I am getting the last laugh, aren't I? Miriam?

MIRIAM: You are not that well-known. You . . .

OSCAR: True, you live in Miami, and Cubans here are totally illiterate.

MIRIAM: Ha!

OSCAR: Ha!

(Oscar embraces her.)

MIRIAM: Don't kiss me.

OSCAR: Your lips have withered.

MIRIAM: So have yours.

OSCAR: Ha.

MIRIAM: Up yours. Ha! When are you leaving?

OSCAR: My plane leaves tomorrow at noon. So I can stay for the whole show.

MIRIAM: Funeral, not a show. It's your grandmother's funeral!

OSCAR: To the end of a tortured life.

MIRIAM: Yes.

(Oscar starts to cry.)

Good. Two in a row.

OSCAR: Fuck you!

MIRIAM: Can't you leave earlier?

OSCAR: No, there's only one flight to Cuba.

MIRIAM: Cuba!

OSCAR: You knew I was going.

MIRIAM: I thought in the future.

OSCAR: No, I've been planning it for months.

MIRIAM: So you didn't come here for her?

OSCAR: No. It just so happened that I had a one-day stopover, when my mother called me with the news.

(Miriam spits at him.)

MIRIAM: Bastard.

OSCAR: She abandoned me, like you all abandoned me. Why should I make a special trip, 'cause she has something in her genes that has something to do with mine.

MIRIAM: You abandoned us.

OSCAR: No, I just didn't become who you wanted me to become. You know there's people in the world that admire me. That look up to me.

MIRIAM: Why are you going to Cuba?!

OSCAR: To forgive him, you, myself. This whole goddamned family. This whole fucking town. To be a part of it. To finally really be a part of my country. My home.

MIRIAM: You are a part of this country.

OSCAR: Miriam . . .

MIRIAM: You are a success.

OSCAR: But it leaves me empty. No, that's not the reason . . . I'm not empty. I don't know who I am.

MIRIAM: You are such a neurotic. In a family full of them, you win the prize.

(Daniel enters.)

OSCAR: I have to find something that saves me. I can't keep living in the past. I'm always this scared kid on an airplane leaving it . . . home . . . island . . . Cu . . . Cu . . . Cojímar . . . Cojí-mar.

(Oscar starts to cry.)

MIRIAM: Don't cry again.

DANIEL: Listen, Cousin. We have an opportunity to bury the past and live here happily.

OSCAR: What would you know? You were born here.

DANIEL: So what?

OSCAR: You're a dentist, right? What would a dentist know about passion?

DANIEL: I'm an architect.

OSCAR: Right. Your father is the one that's a dentist.

DANIEL: Why are you being mean?

OSCAR: 'Cause I jump into emotion.

DANIEL: Is that a virtue?

OSCAR: Yes.

MIRIAM: No!

OSCAR: Jump into life, kid.

DANIEL: I can't.

OSCAR: Why not?

DANIEL: You are making me nervous; please stop.

OSCAR: Why?

DANIEL: I don't know how to jump.

OSCAR: That's tragic.

MIRIAM: My son has a fear of falling.

OSCAR: That's fear of orgasm.

DANIEL: Excuse me? *Hello*, my mother is here.

OSCAR: Are you afraid of letting go in sex?

MIRIAM: Oscar.

OSCAR: What?

MIRIAM: Don't talk about orgasms to my son.

OSCAR: Why? You've had them, I know you have.

DANIEL: How do you know?

OSCAR: I knew her when she was young.

MIRIAM: That's true, I have them.

OSCAR: Everyone in the house could hear you.

MIRIAM: Daniel, when I was young everybody wanted me.

DANIEL: What do you mean?

MIRIAM: Nothing.

OSCAR: She knew how to jump.

DANIEL: What are you saying? How about my dad?

MIRIAM: Everybody wanted me . . .

OSCAR: So don't let her stop you.

DANIEL: She doesn't. I date plenty of girls.

OSCAR: I'm sure you do. Cubans too, I bet.

DANIEL: *La crème de la crème.*

MIRIAM: I was wild. Your mother was wild.

OSCAR: In your way.

MIRIAM: Age is a terrible thing.

OSCAR: I know. It makes you become someone who you really are not.

MIRIAM: You feel old?

OSCAR: Yes.

MIRIAM: If you're having a midlife crisis, buy yourself a Ferrari. I'll forgive you for your books. But don't go to Cuba. Please.

OSCAR: It's time to forgive Fidel, Miriam.

MIRIAM: Never.

OSCAR: It is.

MIRIAM: Never!

OSCAR: I'm going home. I'm going to make peace. Embrace and kiss him.

MIRIAM: He wouldn't kiss you.

OSCAR: He is going to have to.

MIRIAM: He's a monster. Monsters don't learn.

OSCAR: You can't talk me out of this.

MIRIAM: You are going?

OSCAR: Of course.

MIRIAM: Don't ever speak to me again. If you go. Don't ever come to talk to me. Don't ever ask me for anything.

OSCAR: What difference would that make to me? I never speak to you anyway. I'm going to Cuba.

MIRIAM: Not while I am alive.

OSCAR: You cannot stop me.

MIRIAM: I will!

OSCAR: How?

MIRIAM: Son of a bitch. You'll see how.

OSCAR: I have the right to go home. I am going to have my picture taken kissing Fidel. What's the difference between my father and him? Same generation, stubborn, vain, you are all the same!

(Miriam starts to scream.)

MIRIAM: Jesus! Jesus! Jesus Christ! Listen to me! I'm getting your father!

(She exits.)

OSCAR: She's become religious?

DANIEL: Soon she'll start speaking in tongues.

(Oscar laughs.)

OSCAR: That's a good one.

DANIEL: Thanks. Hello.

OSCAR: Hello.

DANIEL: Nice to see you. I've read all your books.

OSCAR: Authentic, aren't they?

DANIEL: Down to the last detail.

OSCAR: That means a lot.

DANIEL: I'm happy to . . .

OSCAR: I have this tape recorder in my head filled with their voices. They never stop. Their stupidity, their greed, their libido. And what they lost. The island. Like a movie that's always playing . . . with a million reels that never end . . . round and round it plays . . . and I write and write, run and run. So I'm just going to go. And face it. Why is that a crime?

DANIEL: Well, we're supposed to boycott, not give a cent. Keep everything closed to him . . .

OSCAR: Yeah, yeah . . .

DANIEL: In order to starve him into submission.

OSCAR: It hasn't worked.

DANIEL: You got to give it time.

OSCAR: It's been more than thirty years.

DANIEL: Even if it takes a hundred.

OSCAR: But we are all drowning from it.

DANIEL: Life is meant for suffering.

OSCAR: Do you really believe that?

DANIEL: Do you?

OSCAR: Unfortunately yes, but I hoped it skipped your generation.

DANIEL: Unfortunately, no such luck.

OSCAR: I think I like you.

DANIEL: You only like people that suffer?

OSCAR: I only like outsiders.

DANIEL: What makes you think I am?

OSCAR: Instinct.

(Daniel laughs nervously.)

Don't be nervous, Cousin.

DANIEL: I'm not!

OSCAR: Good.

DANIEL: Great to meet you again.

(They shake hands.)

OSCAR: Yes.

DANIEL: Right, well . . .

OSCAR: Tell me something will you? Who's in there?

DANIEL: Everyone.

OSCAR: The past.

DANIEL: That's what I told my mother.

OSCAR: Hmm. The past. How can you ever forgive the past?

DANIEL: What?

OSCAR: Nothing, talking to myself. Sorry. You wanted to say something?

DANIEL: I always wanted to meet you again. Last time I saw you I was ten.

OSCAR: You wouldn't happen to have some scotch on you, would you?

DANIEL: Sorry, no.

OSCAR: When I was your age I always carried a flask on occasions like this one.

DANIEL: Good idea.

OSCAR: I'm a failure to them. No matter what I do. I don't measure up to their ideals.

DANIEL: No one does.

OSCAR: It's hard to justify being a fascist in 1994.

DANIEL: What?

OSCAR: That's what they admire, fascists and millionaires.

DANIEL: Your lip is trembling.

OSCAR: Nervous.

DANIEL: You're nervous?

OSCAR: I'm a very sensitive man.

DANIEL: I know that.

OSCAR: Well, do something for me, won't you?

DANIEL: We are first cousins. It's a sin.

OSCAR: What?

DANIEL: I've always been attracted to you. Always. I used to masturbate to your picture. The one where you were wearing the 1940s hat, the one in the back of your second novel. You looked like a gangster and a black and white movie star all at once. But you are my first cousin . . . it's a sin!

OSCAR: Those rules only apply if you are going to have children. But . . .

DANIEL: What are you saying!

OSCAR: I don't want you to suck my cock.

DANIEL: You don't?

OSCAR: Not right now.

DANIEL: Okay. What a relief.

OSCAR: I need a drink. How can there be nothing to sedate one at a funeral?

DANIEL: I can steal a Valium from my mother's purse.

OSCAR: You're a sweetheart. Thanks.

DANIEL: Oh. You're welcome.

OSCAR: Go steal for me.

DANIEL: Okay. Maybe later?

OSCAR: Anything can happen.

DANIEL: You couldn't tell by looking at me, could you?

OSCAR: No, you are *muy macho*.

DANIEL: I practice a manly walk all the time. No one can tell, right?

(He walks up and down in a manly fashion.)

Right?

OSCAR: Absolutely, no one can tell. Only me 'cause I'm so sensitive.

DANIEL: About the subject.

OSCAR: Got a built-in radar.

DANIEL: Why did you get married?

OSCAR: Tradition?

DANIEL: I'm thinking of getting married myself.

(Daniel exits.)

OSCAR *(To himself)*: Silly queen. Because I loved her. Not everything is black and white.

(Oscar takes out a gold pen and a small notebook. He writes. Then reads:)

"If I write 'Please forgive my father' a hundred times. Would I have paid my penance?"

(Yolanda enters.)

YOLANDA: Well, hello Oscar. *(She kisses him politely)* Such a long time.

OSCAR: Hello, hello Tia. Are you all right?

YOLANDA: Of course, it's not my mother that died. You should come in. They're doing a rosary soon.

OSCAR: In a minute.

(He starts to shake.)

Sorry.

YOLANDA: Sit down.

OSCAR: No.

(The shaking gets worse.)

YOLANDA: You're not having a seizure are you?

OSCAR: I haven't had one of those since . . . I was eighteen and the vampire came in, and I said, "Okay, do it." And it felt good.

YOLANDA: The vampire?

OSCAR: Yes. The men with canes were vampires. Don't you remember?

YOLANDA: I thought they were zombies.

OSCAR: They were every fear known to man. I let him bite me. And they never came back. I'm sorry. I cannot stop it. I'm sorry. It must be my body's reaction to Miami.

YOLANDA: Should I get a doctor? Your cousin the doctor is inside . . .

OSCAR: No.

YOLANDA: But.

OSCAR: It's just anxiety and panic.

YOLANDA: About Cuba?

OSCAR: Even at her mother's funeral, Miriam can gossip. And fast.

YOLANDA: Actually, your mother told me and I told her.

OSCAR: My mother is not here, is she?

YOLANDA: No.

OSCAR: Thank God.

YOLANDA: I understand why you think you have to go.

OSCAR: You do?

YOLANDA: To finish a story.

OSCAR: Partly, yes.

YOLANDA: But go quietly please.

OSCAR: Why?

YOLANDA: We have to live in Miami.

OSCAR: I remember when you lived in New York, in Jackson Heights. I remember being stuck with you on the express in the middle of a snow storm.

YOLANDA: Blizzard.

OSCAR: My first.

YOLANDA: Yes.

OSCAR: You remember?

YOLANDA: Yes.

OSCAR: You remember me?

YOLANDA: Of course. I love you.

OSCAR: You do?

YOLANDA: In the blizzard yes . . . we had fun.

OSCAR: I remember your friends there.

YOLANDA: In New York?

OSCAR: Yes.

YOLANDA: You liked them.

OSCAR: They were intelligent. They wrote and painted and went to the theater.

YOLANDA: Why did you turn away from me?

OSCAR: Because you of all people should have understood.

YOLANDA: Understood what?

OSCAR: You tell me.

YOLANDA: Tell you?

OSCAR: Tell me!

YOLANDA: You got jealous when I had my own children, because you were used to being the favorite.

OSCAR: You know who I am.

YOLANDA: No.

OSCAR: You could have saved me.

YOLANDA: From what.

OSCAR: Loneliness at least.

YOLANDA: You're not lonely anymore.

OSCAR: How do you know?

YOLANDA: Men don't allow themselves to get lonely.

OSCAR: Maybe I am not really a man.

YOLANDA: Don't you ever say that.

OSCAR: Maybe I'll always be a boy being sent away alone.

YOLANDA: It's been thirty years, it's time to get over that.

OSCAR: It's been thirty years, it's time to end the embargo.

YOLANDA: Don't you dare start talking about that.

(Miriam and Daniel enter.)

OSCAR: Where is my father?

DANIEL: Praying.

MIRIAM: You could have asked me for a Valium. I would have given it to you. You don't have to sneak one.

OSCAR: So generous with your drugs.

MIRIAM: They're not drugs. They're legal. They're medicine.

YOLANDA: He hasn't stopped shaking.

MIRIAM: Guilt.

OSCAR: Never.

MIRIAM: Remorse.

OSCAR: Why?

MIRIAM: Why!

DANIEL: I'll get you water.

(Daniel goes to get water.)

MIRIAM: You know when he was a kid, he loved you. My son.

OSCAR: Why? I didn't know him.

MIRIAM: When you were in *Time* magazine, he put the photo up on his wall.

OSCAR: I heard.

MIRIAM: What?

OSCAR: He told me a minute ago. Very sweet, your son.

MIRIAM: And very handsome and extremely manly.

OSCAR: Like his mamá.

MIRIAM: Very funny.

OSCAR: But true.

MIRIAM: I guess what I am trying to say is that . . .

YOLANDA: For better or for worse we are your family.

MIRIAM: So don't turn your grandmother's funeral, who you didn't speak to for twenty years into . . .

OSCAR: She never called me.

MIRIAM: She didn't know your number.

OSCAR: Miriam!

YOLANDA: Call her Tia.

OSCAR: Tia Miriam. You gotta be kidding. Didn't know my number!

MIRIAM: All I am saying is, keep the Cuba crap to yourself. Tonight.

OSCAR: Where is my water!

DANIEL: Here.

(Oscar takes the Valium.)

MIRIAM: Now go inside.

YOLANDA: Yes.

OSCAR: No.

YOLANDA: Come on.

OSCAR: No. I have an embargo against that room. We don't agree ideologically about life. So I will not enter the room. Till there are no differences between us.

MIRIAM: The rosary is starting soon. You can kneel. Pray. And not talk.

OSCAR: No.

YOLANDA: Do a rosary and you'll feel better.

OSCAR: No.

MIRIAM: My mother's life was destroyed by communism. I won't let you ruin her funeral with that same bullshit.

YOLANDA: Please, Oscar; pay your respects to your grandmother.

OSCAR: Who am I!

YOLANDA: You were the most polite little boy I ever knew.

OSCAR: Then why did you let them send me away on Peter Pan . . .

MIRIAM: You were not Peter Pan!

OSCAR: Yes, I was. That was the visa they sent me on.

MIRIAM: But I was here waiting for you. You did not go to an orphanage.

OSCAR: You were worse than an orphanage.

MIRIAM: Bastard.

YOLANDA: Stop it!

OSCAR: You told me my parents were never going to come here.

YOLANDA: How could you, Miriam?

MIRIAM: I was young.

YOLANDA: You were mean.

MIRIAM: I was only twenty-one. I was confused.

YOLANDA: But you took it out on a child?

MIRIAM: Leave me alone.

YOLANDA: What else did she tell you?

MIRIAM: I locked him out of the house.

YOLANDA: I see.

MIRIAM: I was young, I was broke, I was alone. Don't judge me. You were not here at the beginning, Yolanda. So don't judge me.

DANIEL: Poor Mamá.

MIRIAM: It's all so sad.

OSCAR: Yes, it is.

YOLANDA: That's exile.

DANIEL: Yes, it is.

YOLANDA: That's what that bastard did to us.

DANIEL: Fidel.

YOLANDA: Yes.

MIRIAM: Maybe.

OSCAR: Sometimes I think we did it to ourselves.

YOLANDA: Never.

(Yolanda exits.)

OSCAR: It wasn't all his fault, and you know that.

MIRIAM: It was.

DANIEL: All his fault?

MIRIAM: Absolutely. Fidel destroyed our family.

OSCAR: How can you be so sure?

MIRIAM: Because my life depends on it.

OSCAR: Not mine.

MIRIAM: Lucky you.

OSCAR: Yes.

MIRIAM: I'll see you inside.

OSCAR: I am staying out here.

MIRIAM: Why?

OSCAR: He doesn't want me with him.

MIRIAM: Who?

OSCAR: Your brother.

MIRIAM: The rosary is starting soon.

(Miriam exits.)

OSCAR: Now they're worried.

DANIEL: Good.

OSCAR: You're enjoying this?

DANIEL: Hypocrites, liars.

OSCAR: He who is without sin cast the first stone.

DANIEL: What?

OSCAR: Everybody is a hypocrite, everybody is a liar.

DANIEL: Including you?

OSCAR: And you.

DANIEL: I love your books.

OSCAR: They're not me.

DANIEL: You wrote them.

OSCAR: Yes, I did.

DANIEL: They have insight.

OSCAR: But they are not me.

DANIEL: Oh.

OSCAR: They're all of us.

DANIEL: How can you remember Cuba so clearly?

OSCAR: Because, because. Because . . . Because it's the only happiness I've known.

DANIEL: What?

OSCAR: Fiction.

DANIEL: There has to be a way to be happy.

OSCAR: Is that what you are looking for?

DANIEL: Yes.

OSCAR: Then it's good that you are an architect. That you can define structure.

DANIEL: Sometimes.

OSCAR: You want to be stable?

DANIEL: Sometimes.

OSCAR: You want to be destroyed.

DANIEL: Yes, like the people in your novels.

OSCAR: While I lived in fiction and you learned to build shopping malls, we were both blind to our country. And it's hungry now. Hungry and dying and the houses are falling down. And it does not matter anymore whose fault it is. And if I can make them see that it's time to forgive, if I can convince the people in there praying . . . It will mean more than any novel I have ever read or written. Or any woman or man I have ever wanted, or gotten. I don't want us to be blind, Daniel. I want us—for once—to see clearly. Daniel, help me.

DANIEL: I hate Cuba.

OSCAR: What!

DANIEL: I don't want it to have anything to do with me.

OSCAR: Why do you like my novels?

DANIEL: Because of the sex.
OSCAR: Really?
DANIEL: Because of the incest.
OSCAR: That's just a subplot.

(Oscar takes out a cigar case.)

DANIEL: Not to me.

(Oscar cuts a cigar with a cigar cutter.)

OSCAR: Want one? Cuban!
DANIEL: Never!
OSCAR: Never say never.

(He starts to light the cigar.)

DANIEL: Don't smoke those terrible cigars, please.
OSCAR: Our heritage.

(The cigar goes out.)

DANIEL: I'm glad you can't light it.

(He starts to light it.)

OSCAR: You have to keep sucking to get it to stay alive.
DANIEL: You'll never light it.

(Yolanda enters.
Daniel exits.)

YOLANDA: He's not happy.
OSCAR: Yes he is.
YOLANDA: What?
OSCAR: He loves to act miserable. He is Miriam's son. He's cursed.
YOLANDA: I don't think he's acting.

OSCAR: What do you want?

YOLANDA: People are wondering why you haven't come in.

OSCAR: Tell them.

YOLANDA: If anyone in that room hears that you are going to Cuba, they will hate you forever. My uncle . . .

OSCAR: Which one?

YOLANDA: The one that was in jail for twenty-eight years.

OSCAR: You are not going to make me feel guilty.

YOLANDA: He was naked in a jail for ten of those years.

OSCAR: I know this story. I know it!

YOLANDA: He was tortured.

OSCAR: Yes! I know!

YOLANDA: He died a year after they let him out. His life was stolen.

OSCAR: I told you. I know!

YOLANDA: Beaten out of him. By the man you want to kiss.

OSCAR: I don't want to kiss him.

YOLANDA: Now you're thinking straight.

OSCAR: But I have to kiss him.

YOLANDA: What the hell for! What the hell for!

OSCAR: So it ends.

YOLANDA: So what ends?

OSCAR: The separation between us.

YOLANDA: Fidel separated us.

OSCAR: No, we left.

YOLANDA: Because he took our property.

OSCAR: Life has to mean more than property.

YOLANDA: It doesn't.

OSCAR: It has to!

YOLANDA: He took away our faith.

OSCAR: Life has to mean more than faith.

YOLANDA: Not possible. Faith is everything. Have you forgotten the mysteries of Christ?

(Miriam has entered.)

MIRIAM: You are trying to be rational with someone who is brainwashed. It won't work.

OSCAR: The only people that washed my brain were you. My family. All the shit you wanted me to believe.

MIRIAM: What shit?

OSCAR: That you were victims. You weren't victims.

MIRIAM: We were not responsible.

OSCAR: You knew about the corruption, you profited from Batista's dictatorship. You did!

MIRIAM: Well, so what!

YOLANDA: Yes, so what! Who didn't!

OSCAR: *¿Por qué me has hecho sufrir tanto tia?*

MIRIAM: She didn't make you suffer.

YOLANDA: *Porque el mundo se acabo.*

OSCAR: No, Tia. No.

YOLANDA: *El dia que uno de nosotros. Que uno de los nuestros vaya a hablar con un comunista.*

OSCAR: *No soy coño. No soy comunista.*

YOLANDA: *Estoy trantando de . . .*

OSCAR: *Desde que tengo diez y nueve años no he existido más para ti.*

YOLANDA: *¿Qué quieres?*

OSCAR: *¿Que entiendas la verdad?*

MIRIAM: Fuck the truth.

OSCAR: Fuck is such an easy word to say in English.

YOLANDA: Fidel is a communist, goddamn you!

(Yolanda hits him. He pushes her away.)

OSCAR: *AAY! Aay. Hombres con bastones. ¡Ay me quieren cortar la cabeza! ¡Se estan comiendo mi pipi! ¡Ay tia ay!*

(Daniel enters.)

DANIEL: Oscar?

OSCAR: *Salvame.*

DANIEL: Save you? I can't save you.

MIRIAM: He's not talking to you.

OSCAR: *Hombres con bastones. Se estan comiendo mi pipi.*

DANIEL: Men with big sticks are eating your penis? What is it with you?

MIRIAM: He is going to that other place.

DANIEL: You've seen him do this before?

YOLANDA: His entire childhood.

DANIEL: Poor baby.

(Oscar starts to shake and collapses in Daniel's arms.)

MIRIAM: You're strong to hold him like that, Son.

DANIEL: Maybe.

YOLANDA: *Comemierda.*

MIRIAM: I knew he was suffering underneath.

YOLANDA: So did I. She is his grandmother.

MIRIAM: When he wakes up, he'll be ours again.

YOLANDA: He'll see her in his vision.

DANIEL: Who?

MIRIAM: My mother.

YOLANDA: Yes, and she'll tell him the embargo is forever. Because it is. I'll see how the guests are doing.

MIRIAM: Thank you, Yolanda.

YOLANDA: Sure.

(Yolanda exits.)

DANIEL: Oscar?

(Oscar comes to.)

OSCAR: Hold me. Comfort me. My lips . . . kiss my lips. Tia? Family life was comforting. Your kisses. Nothing I put into my mouth gives me comfort.

DANIEL: You collapsed in my arms.

(Oscar kisses Daniel's neck. Then Daniel's hand.)

OSCAR: Daniel. Cousin.

DANIEL: Yes?

OSCAR: Why don't we show her who we really are?

DANIEL: How?

OSCAR: Kiss me.

DANIEL: Kiss you?

OSCAR: Yes?

DANIEL: Now?

OSCAR: Yes.

DANIEL: No. No thank you.

(Oscar faints.)

MIRIAM: Son, get away from him!

(Yolanda walks back in with coffee cups.)

YOLANDA: They asked for more café.

MIRIAM: Well, we have to stay up all night.

YOLANDA: Has he said anything else?

DANIEL: He is out.

MIRIAM: Again.

YOLANDA: Good.

DANIEL: I'm going to call an ambulance.

MIRIAM: A doctor won't help him.

DANIEL: Why?

MIRIAM: It's mystical, not physical.

YOLANDA: The beyond. He's having another vision.

DANIEL: You really believe in all that stuff?

YOLANDA: It's your grandmother calling him. He always had the gift.

DANIEL: But he feels so cold.

MIRIAM: This is the way it happened when he was little.

DANIEL: Are you sure?

YOLANDA: He was always cold. When he entered the other world.

DANIEL: What do you mean?

MIRIAM: He's seeing things.

YOLANDA: Let's go. His grandmother will take care of it all.

DANIEL: But he has fainted.

MIRIAM: Daniel, take care of him.

YOLANDA: Call me when he comes back from the dead.

DANIEL: Sure.

(They exit.)

Come back, Oscar. Come back to me. I don't want you to live in the past.

(Oscar comes to.)

OSCAR: The past is a jail!

DANIEL: You're awake.

OSCAR: I heard your voice.

DANIEL: I am thinking of going to Cuba with you.

OSCAR: I thought you didn't care about Cuba?

DANIEL: I care about you.

OSCAR: I don't trust you.

DANIEL: I want to go home to Cuba.

OSCAR: Home?

DANIEL: Yes! Home. Our home.

(Oscar starts to shake.)

OSCAR: But you're not from the soil . . . you're not on the inside *(Shaking violently)*. I know the in and the outs, and the how and the why nots, and the longing . . . And the fucking regrets . . . And all the unrequited tropical fishes that died from being overfed in the tank . . . In the dark when the men with black canes and the silver tips come and poke at my flesh . . . I know the whole story and they hate me for that . . . but I swore a secret code . . . and if I ever tell . . . I will never go home . . . I will never go home . . . I will die all alone. If I tell, it's exile for me for the rest of my days.

(He faints again on Daniel.)

DANIEL: Jesus, is this fair? Tom is tall and muscular and blonde and you are falling apart. I'm in love with a guy who's begun to lose all his hair.

*(Daniel kisses Oscar on the lips.
    Blackout.)*

ACT TWO

It is an hour later. Oscar is still on the floor. Daniel is holding him. Miriam and Yolanda enter.

YOLANDA: Should I get his father?
DANIEL: What for? I'm here.

(Daniel goes to pour a cup of café.)

MIRIAM: What do you mean?
YOLANDA: Daniel, you didn't call me.
DANIEL: I have to give Oscar some first.
YOLANDA: Why?
DANIEL: Like Grandma, she always gave him café after an attack. I am going to take care of him.
YOLANDA: You are going to be his nurse?
DANIEL: No.
YOLANDA: His assistant?
DANIEL: Do I look like an assistant?
OSCAR: Where am I?
DANIEL: Hell.

OSCAR: Right, Miami.

DANIEL: Right.

OSCAR: Daniel? Why are you being so nice?

DANIEL: I feel very close to you. We are going to Cuba together remember!

OSCAR: Right.

DANIEL: Good.

OSCAR: What a giving cousin.

DANIEL: Kissing cousins?

OSCAR: That sounds possible.

(Daniel plays with Oscar's hair.)

DANIEL: You still got some left.

OSCAR: Do I?

YOLANDA: I don't approve, Oscar. I don't approve.

OSCAR: You mean you never slept with all those dykes you had as friends?

YOLANDA: Dykes?

OSCAR: Those painters in Jackson Heights.

YOLANDA: They were old maids!

OSCAR: You never kissed them?

YOLANDA: Who do you think you are talking to?

MIRIAM: Did my mother's ghost appear to you in the vision?

OSCAR: What?

YOLANDA: You started seeing the men with canes again. Didn't you?

OSCAR: What?

MIRIAM: They came back. Remember?

OSCAR: They did?

YOLANDA: Yes.

MIRIAM: Don't you remember?

OSCAR: Yes. Oh my God, they came back. See what you do to me? You haunt me!

MIRIAM: What did they tell you?

YOLANDA: Where did they take you?

MIRIAM: Did my mother speak to you?

YOLANDA: Did she warn you against going to Cuba?

OSCAR: I see them . . . I remember now . . . they surrounded me . . . They say, "We are waiting for you in Cuba" . . . "What?" I tell them. It all goes dark. They take out their canes. They start poking me with their sharp silver tips. One of them pokes at my lips. I bleed, my mouth bleeds. The lights come up and I know we are in purgatory. Because Pedro is there.

MIRIAM: Pedro.

YOLANDA: Your uncle?

OSCAR: Yes, his throat is full of stitches and he tells me he can not go to heaven, till I go home and face it all.

MIRIAM: You're lying.

OSCAR: Face it all.

YOLANDA: What the hell is "all"?

OSCAR: The street, the house, the room upstairs, the cemetery where his wife laid intact for decades. "La Terraza," where we all ate paella and looked down at the poor, who were sitting at the bar having one beer. "La Floridita," where Grandpa sat and drank daiquiris and betrayed Grandma with showgirls. Where the blood was spilled for the revolution on every street corner. That I have to smell the blood on the streets . . . and when I finally do smell it . . . I must drive to Varadero, walk on the white sand by the "Dupont Mansion," go into the ocean and be blessed by Yemaya, and float in peace and joy . . . if I did all that, the stitches around his throat will disappear and the pain will evaporate. Miriam, your mother was not there.

DANIEL: She must have gone straight to heaven.

MIRIAM: I doubt it.

YOLANDA: Miriam, don't say that.

MIRIAM: So they told you to go to Cuba, how convenient for you.

OSCAR: You wanted to know.

YOLANDA: That's not the vision we were hoping for.

OSCAR: No? Too bad.

YOLANDA: Are sure it was not your mind just playing tricks on you.

OSCAR: I saw Pedro clear as day.

MIRIAM: What was he wearing?

OSCAR: His pajamas. He had shaving cream on his face. He was holding a straight razor in one of his hands, his left hand.

(Yolanda crosses herself.)

YOLANDA: Pedro was left handed.

MIRIAM: Shut up. You should be ashamed Oscar. Playing with the dead for your own self-interest.

OSCAR: What self-interest?

MIRIAM: When you betray us by going to Cuba.

YOLANDA: That's right, if you go there you are betraying the living and the dead.

MIRIAM: Both sides of your family.

OSCAR: I am sorry.

YOLANDA: My father, who died in exile.

MIRIAM: Your grandmother, who we are going to bury in exile, generations of Cubans who have lived and died longing to go home. But who have known that their duty is to fight him. Fight the son of a bitch!

OSCAR: I'm sorry.

YOLANDA: Your duty is to fight Fidel, not kiss him.

OSCAR: I'm sorry. God, you make me feel . . .

MIRIAM: Guilty?

OSCAR: Yes.

YOLANDA: Good.

DANIEL: You're feeling guilty?

OSCAR: A little.

DANIEL: Darling, don't.

YOLANDA: Are you ever going to marry again, Oscar?

OSCAR: No.

YOLANDA: Did your wife break your heart?

OSCAR: I broke hers.

YOLANDA: How?

OSCAR: I left her for a man.

YOLANDA: You can stop being a homosexual. You have to go to a psychiatrist. And be cured. I hear electroshock therapy works!

OSCAR: I don't want to be cured.

YOLANDA: Don't say that! *Virgen de la Caridad*, help us!

(Yolanda begins to cry.)

OSCAR: Jesus Christ! Shit!

YOLANDA: It's a tragedy. Your life is a tragedy. I wish you were dead.

OSCAR: I want men. All the time. I want them to fill me up.

DANIEL: Don't be graphic, please.

OSCAR: Why not?

DANIEL: 'Cause I know you are really a romantic.

OSCAR: Really?

MIRIAM: You don't have to be so vulgar.

DANIEL: I know you believe in love.

OSCAR: Do I?

DANIEL: I know you do.

OSCAR: It's time to forgive Fidel.

(We hear someone singing a Hail Mary.)

Fuck! That noise!

MIRIAM: They're doing the rosary. Your father hired someone to sing it.

YOLANDA: Singing keeps people awake. "Our Fathers" and "Ave Marias" sung.

MIRIAM: It's very in. In high society.

(Oscar goes and stands in front of the door leading to the funeral.)

OSCAR: Stop the fucking noise, Dad!

MIRIAM: Well. Look at my brother's face.

OSCAR: Come in here and let's have a debate. I am going to Cuba. I am going to have café with Fidel. I am going to have my picture taken with him. I am going to embrace him. I am going to be friends with the son of a bitch!

DANIEL: Oh, God!

(Osvaldo enters.)

OSVALDO: Enough! Go home! Before I take off my belt.

(Daniel runs out into the room.)

MIRIAM: Let the fighting begin.

OSCAR: And hit me?

OSVALDO: Teach you how to show respect!

MIRIAM: Good, Osvaldo.

OSVALDO: Either act like a good son or leave.

OSCAR: I don't know how to be a good son.

OSVALDO: Act the part.

OSCAR: A nice little Cuban?

OSVALDO: No more Cuba bullshit. Cuba is gone it's as simple as that.

MIRIAM: No, it's not!

OSVALDO: For me it is.

YOLANDA: Never! Cuba is always right in front of my face.

OSVALDO: Not mine.

MIRIAM: That's 'cause you left Miami!

YOLANDA: You lost yourself in L.A!

OSVALDO: No, I found myself.

OSCAR: You know who you are?

OSVALDO: Yes.

OSCAR: So do I. I am the one that's going back.

OSVALDO: No son of mine makes peace with the enemy, with the dictator, with that son of a bitch . . .

OSCAR: Well, I am.

(Daniel rushes back in.)

DANIEL: Everybody is talking. A couple of them want to beat you up!

OSVALDO: I wish they would.

OSCAR: I'm going to let them all know what I think.

DANIEL: They really do want to beat you up!

OSCAR: Bring them on.

OSVALDO: Suddenly you are macho?

OSCAR: Yes!

OSVALDO: I'm going into the other room. And I don't want to see you again today.

OSCAR: Don't you love me?

OSVALDO: I loved the other you.

OSCAR: Who is that?

OSVALDO: The good son. The one who knew Fidel betrayed us.

OSCAR: He died years ago.

OSVALDO: And you survived.

OSCAR: Yes.

OSVALDO: How sad.

OSCAR: Yes.

(Osvaldo starts to go. Oscar screams after him.)

You exploited the working class, that's the reason we had a revolution, because we made money out of their sweat. Because you thought we owned the world.

(Osvaldo exits. Miriam slams the door shut and exits. Oscar goes to the door but it's locked.)

That bitch.

YOLANDA: It's so easy for you.

OSCAR: No it's not.

YOLANDA: Listen to me, goddammit! You walked away. You think you are trapped in it, in the past, but you walked away. To a life that can only be lived in the streets of Manhattan and in rooms filled with writers. How can you be rational? Our lives ended the day Fidel took over our bus company. Our father died that day. I saw his spirit disappear forever. We came here, thought we'd go back, but never did. I married a man I did not love, and you became a pervert. All that happened because of Fidel Castro. Because of the goddamn revolution.

OSCAR: I was me long before the revolution. You made me. Cuba made me.

(We hear a police siren. Miriam runs in.)

MIRIAM: Why are the police here?

YOLANDA: Oh my God, the police. Has there been an accident?

OSCAR: Jesus, will you two relax?

DANIEL: Are you carrying illegal drugs?

OSCAR: No.

DANIEL: Are you sure?

OSCAR: Positive.

YOLANDA: Good.

OSCAR: Are you, Daniel?

DANIEL: I never do drugs.

(Miriam has been looking out a window.)

MIRIAM: They are walking towards this funeral home. What do we do?

OSCAR: Architect, take care of it.

DANIEL: Why?

OSCAR: You're the most normal person here.

DANIEL: Thank you, Oscar.

MIRIAM: Stop flirting with my son.

(Daniel goes out.)

YOLANDA: What kind of trouble have you brought to us?

OSCAR: Reality.

MIRIAM: That's high and mighty of you.

YOLANDA: What do the police want?

OSCAR: To send us back?

YOLANDA: I'm an American citizen.

OSCAR: And they need every Republican vote they can get in Florida.

YOLANDA: Maybe they're coming to send you back.

OSCAR: I'm part of their cultural elite.

YOLANDA: Exactly.

(Daniel enters with another young man, Ismael. Ismael has a shaved head. He is sunburned and very dirty.)

ISMAEL: ¿La familia?

MIRIAM: Who the hell is that?

OSCAR: *¿Quién eres?*

ISMAEL: Talk to me in English. I have to practice the lingo if I'm gonna be a gringo.

OSCAR: Who are you?

ISMAEL: Ismael. I'm your cousin Fernando's son.

MIRIAM: Ismael Ruiz?

ISMAEL: Yes.

MIRIAM: The crazy one?

ISMAEL: Crazy but happy! Yo!

OSCAR: A new cousin?

ISMAEL: *Dios mio. La familia*, my cousins!

OSCAR: Ismael, Cousin. My God, you are sun burned.

DANIEL: And he stinks.

OSCAR: Quiet.

MIRIAM: How did you get out?

ISMAEL: A raft from Cojímar. I was at sea six days.

OSCAR: What?

DANIEL: He left on a raft.

ISMAEL: Made out of old bus tires and wood. I made it.

OSCAR: How did you learn English?

ISMAEL: School. Records. John Lennon.

OSCAR: Smart.

ISMAEL: I could not live there anymore. Life is like jail there. They hate me 'cause I love hip hop. My rhymes are too heavy. They drop on the man like Playa Girón.

DANIEL: "Life is like a jail there. They hate hip hop."

OSCAR: No, they hate him because he loves hip hop.

DANIEL: Shallow reasons for leaving.

OSCAR: Maybe it's a metaphor.

ISMAEL: Rock 'n' roll taught me English. But now I'm a gangsta. Represent C to the U to the B- A. Wha!

OSCAR: What?

MIRIAM: What language is he talking?

YOLANDA: They brainwashed him. See, that's what Cuba is like.

ISMAEL: Thug for life. I say whatever the fuck I want to say through my rhymes. Thug for life, bitch!

OSCAR: You're the kind of relative I've been waiting for.

DANIEL: Are you trying to hurt me?

YOLANDA: He sounds like a black man.

ISMAEL: Who are you?

YOLANDA: Yolanda.

OSCAR: My mother's sister.

ISMAEL: Claro. Yolanda Garcia.

YOLANDA: He knows all about us.

MIRIAM: I think they spend all their time talking about us.

YOLANDA: Maybe.

MIRIAM: How did you find us?

ISMAEL: The police took me to your house . . . You're my family . . . you are responsible for me . . . word?

MIRIAM: I know. I know. But how did you find the funeral home?

ISMAEL: Your maid told us the tragic news . . . Your mother, my great-aunt. I always wanted to meet her . . .

MIRIAM: Yes, yes, right.

OSCAR: Welcome, welcome, Ismael.

ISMAEL: You got my back, Cousin. You're an artist. Straight up.

DANIEL: Do you play any instruments?

ISMAEL: I'm a rapper. If I had some decks, I would scratch, yo . . . Wick wickedy wick wick . . . But all they got is drums.

DANIEL: The drums.

MIRIAM: That's noisy.

ISMAEL: I am a revolutionary. In my concert, I take a big picture of Fidel and I take out my thing and I piss on his face. So they threw me in jail. But I have liberated myself from him. I've come to America, where you can play music and say whatever the fuck you want and piss on anybody. Word?

OSCAR: Maybe.

DANIEL: I really wouldn't know.

ISMAEL: I am part of the family at last.

OSCAR: Yes.

DANIEL: Sure.

ISMAEL: I read your books. I loved everything about them. *Primo.*

(Oscar embraces Ismael.)

OSCAR: *Te amo.*

ISMAEL: Very friendly. Yes?

OSCAR: You want to say what you want to say and that's it. That's all. That is what I've done my whole life.

ISMAEL: But no one told you not to say what you wanted say.

OSCAR: What?

ISMAEL: You have not been censored.

OSCAR: I have. I have not been allowed to go home. The same way you came here. Now I'm going there.

ISMAEL: Where?

OSCAR: Cuba.

ISMAEL: What for? You don't know what it is like to live without liberty.

YOLANDA: Well said.

ISMAEL: We are starving there.

YOLANDA: I know.

DANIEL: Because of the embargo.

ISMAEL: Because Fidel is a tyrant.

YOLANDA: I love this boy.

ISMAEL: It's whack, yo. They want to arrest me 'cause my rhymes be like crimes . . .

OSCAR: I thought it was because you take your prick out in public.

ISMAEL: As a political act.

OSCAR: They'd arrest you for that here also.

ISMAEL: Word? Nah! I'm hungry.

MIRIAM: I'll send someone to buy him a sandwich.

ISMAEL: I have sold myself to German tourists for a sandwich.

YOLANDA: What does he mean?

MIRIAM: He's a hooker.

YOLANDA: No!

DANIEL: Men or women?

ISMAEL: Both.

DANIEL: Wow.

ISMAEL: It was worth it. To eat.

MIRIAM: Fidel reduced our family to whoring.

YOLANDA: And you still want to go there! Oscar?

ISMAEL: Want to get ahead. Gotta give some head. Know what I mean?

OSCAR: No.

ISMAEL: You must, you're an artist.

DANIEL: Head?

OSCAR: No, I don't. I sold my talent, not my body.

(Ismael grabs his crotch.)

ISMAEL: In communism this was all I could sell.

YOLANDA: Let's not talk about this anymore.

MIRIAM: Your hair will grow out. You'll stay out of the sun. You'll be white again. A couple of baths, you won't stink anymore . . .

ISMAEL: The men I find are easier to seduce than the women. Easier to get. The women want romance. But the men, you just hang out in front of the Ferrari dealership. They offer to buy you a beer. You grab their hand, you put it here . . .

(Ismael takes Oscar's hand, puts it on his belly button.)

And you say that's the head of my cock and it's not even hard. You know what I'm saying?

DANIEL: That's repulsive.

OSCAR: I know what you're saying. Forgive us.

ISMAEL: I am so tired. I have been awake for six days. Gotta take a snooze. Or I lose. Snick snickedy snooze . . .

(Ismael drops to the floor.)

MIRIAM: Not on the floor, no! He's going to dirty the tiles.

DANIEL: Let him sleep on the floor, Mama.

MIRIAM: We have to clean him up, my guests cannot see a cousin of mine looking like this.

DANIEL: But he escaped the tyrant.

MIRIAM: That's not a reason to smell.

(Ismael is now asleep.)

YOLANDA: The boys should take his clothes off.

MIRIAM: Yes.

DANIEL: So the guests can see him naked?

OSCAR: Maybe after they see the size of his cock they'll want to give him a job.

YOLANDA: Don't be vulgar.

MIRIAM: The mortician sells suits for the corpses and paper shoes. We'll dress him in that.

YOLANDA: Yes!

MIRIAM: Come with me to the mortician's office.

YOLANDA: Of course.

MIRIAM: Son. Take his clothes off. Wait till I get disposable gloves.

(Yolanda and Miriam exit.)

OSCAR: Why would they have disposable gloves?

DANIEL: For when they touch a dead body.

(Daniel goes to look for the gloves.)

OSCAR: We lost. They won. We left, they stayed. They're destroying themselves. And we have to go back and be kind. You understand that, right?

(They take off Ismael's clothes.)

DANIEL: In a way, yes. I do. He sold himself for a sandwich.

OSCAR: Because of the embargo, don't you see?

DANIEL: He is beautiful. After we clean him up. He'll look like one of us.

OSCAR: We have forced them to be whores. Don't you see?

DANIEL: I really want to kiss him.

OSCAR: Do it.

DANIEL: Will I get a disease?

OSCAR: Maybe.

DANIEL: It's worth it.

(Daniel kisses Ismael. Miriam and Yolanda walk in.)

OSCAR: Danger is a very exciting thing.

DANIEL: You kiss him now.

YOLANDA: Miriam, put an end to this now.

MIRIAM: Heavens knows anything goes. Right, Oscar?

OSCAR: God, you are sophisticated.

YOLANDA: But I am not.

OSCAR: I was being sarcastic.

YOLANDA: Oscar, what the hell is going on?

OSCAR: We have to save them, not abuse them. Don't you see, the embargo makes us abuse our own families . . .

DANIEL: Mamá, I wanted to kiss him. I have something to say, Mamá. I'm a homosexual.

MIRIAM: I know.

DANIEL: What!

OSCAR: Don't you see that's why we have to end it?

MIRIAM: I am not a fool.

OSCAR: Oh, please. Family, listen to me . . .

DANIEL: Let me confess?

OSCAR: In the middle of my political statement?

DANIEL: Fuck your political statement. I'm coming out to my mother. I'm telling her. Never thought I'd do it.

OSCAR: Stay in the closet if you want. Why should I care? I have something meaningful to say. Without politics we're lost.

YOLANDA: Are you a Democrat, Daniel?

MIRIAM: No, he's not.

DANIEL: Yes I am, Mamá.

MIRIAM: Shit! A faggot and a Democrat.

YOLANDA: Sorry.

DANIEL: It's time she faced reality.

OSCAR: Yes it is.

YOLANDA: Stay out of this.

MIRIAM: I thought you were a Republican. I want my son to be a Republican! And I want you to get married.

OSCAR: Who cares! A Democrat is just a Republican with a guilty conscience.

MIRIAM: Get married soon.

DANIEL: I just told you I was—

MIRIAM: Plenty of faggots get married. Keep a guy on the side.

DANIEL: Mamá, I'm a gay Latino and proud of it!

YOLANDA: Proud?

OSCAR: Good, so let's talk radical politics—

DANIEL: I came out to my mother for you.

OSCAR: That's sweet. Now, back to why the embargo is—

DANIEL: I want you to notice me.

OSCAR: When we get to Cuba, I will.

MIRIAM: You are not going to Cuba with him.

DANIEL: Yes, I am.

MIRIAM: You are corrupting my son.

OSCAR: Like you corrupted me.

MIRIAM: Yes . . . So?

YOLANDA: I've had enough. Cover him up.

(Yolanda throws the suit at Oscar.
    Yolanda exits.)

MIRIAM: You can tell she's not one of us. Doesn't like a fight.

OSCAR: True.

MIRIAM: Too bad.

OSCAR: Yes, not interesting, that's why she never made it into one
    of my books.

MIRIAM: But I did.

OSCAR: Yes, you did.

MIRIAM: Kiss me.

OSCAR: For old time's sake?

MIRIAM: Why not?

OSCAR: Why not.

(They kiss.)

DANIEL: No! Stop it! Fuck this fucking family. Look at me! Oscar!
    I'm handsome. I'm an architect. In this family, you have to be
    a genius or a psychotic or a nympho to be noticed. How can

you kiss her! How come only corruption is interesting? Stop, Mamá, or I'll, or I'll . . .

(Daniel starts to cry.)

MIRIAM: Jealous?
DANIEL: Yes, I am.
MIRIAM: He's a very good kisser, isn't he?
DANIEL: Is he?
OSCAR: All technique.
MIRIAM: What?
OSCAR: Sometimes technique can pass for passion.
MIRIAM: So that was only technique?
OSCAR: That's right.
MIRIAM: Zero desire?
OSCAR: Zero.
MIRIAM: Do you just hate women?
OSCAR: No.
MIRIAM: I think you do. You're not that good a kisser.
OSCAR: I just wanted to please you.
MIRIAM: My husband kisses just fine.
DANIEL: Mamá. He is your nephew! And he's mine!
OSCAR: I'm not yours.
DANIEL: Are you hers?
OSCAR: Maybe.

(Daniel cries.)

MIRIAM: When he was fourteen, he came on vacation, he was reading books all the time. They were by an English man. One night by the pool, he read to me from . . . What was the name of that book?
OSCAR: *Women In Love.*
MIRIAM: Yes, he read to me from *Women In Love*, and every line was like a glass of warm brandy. There were other women like me in the world. The story gave me something strong and sensual that I could hold onto.

DANIEL: He read you the whole book?

MIRIAM: Every night for a week.

OSCAR: Yes. That's right.

MIRIAM: The book told me to give your cousin everything.

DANIEL: Everything?

MIRIAM: Everything.

OSCAR: Books have that kind of power.

MIRIAM: Yes they do.

DANIEL: Oh my God!

OSCAR: It was wonderful to read to you.

MIRIAM: It was?

OSCAR: It was a great summer.

MIRIAM: See, we have shared some good things.

OSCAR: Yes we have.

(Oscar takes Miriam's hand.)

My beautiful aunt.

DANIEL: Why did you have to tell me?

MIRIAM: I thought you loved the truth.

DANIEL: Is he my father, my father?

MIRIAM: Absolutely not. He was fifteen when I had you. What kind of woman do you think I am?

DANIEL: Enough!

MIRIAM: Okay.

DANIEL: I need to say good-bye to Grandma.

MIRIAM: She'd like that.

DANIEL: Are you coming with me? Mamá?

MIRIAM: In a minute. Put the suit on him, Oscar.

OSCAR: By myself?

DANIEL: We can't have a naked man in the middle of a funeral.

(They leave. Oscar starts to dress Ismael, who is still asleep. Oscar talks to him.)

OSCAR: She kissed me one night, my aunt, or did I kiss her? We kissed each other. We needed each other. To make D.H. Lawrence a reality. Did I ruin her? Or were we always ruined? This family defined us, and there was never a way out of the honey comb. Or is there? It's going to take more than soap and water to get rid of your smell.

(He puts the rest of the suit on him.)

Most people think it's all about technique, french kissing. But most people do not realize that it's just giving in. That it's simple: making your lips soft, giving into another person's breath. That's when it's real.

(Oscar relights his cigar.)

This is a Monte Cristo from Havana, Cousin. It never lets me forget. You'll see. Cousin. You'll see what it's really like to leave.

(Daniel enters.)

DANIEL: You are like a vampire.
OSCAR: Really?
DANIEL: You suck in everything about us. Out of us!
OSCAR: I do?
DANIEL: And then you spit it out on a page!
OSCAR: Spit it out?
DANIEL: Yes.
OSCAR: That's not quite it.
DANIEL: Yes it is.
OSCAR: No.
DANIEL: What do you do then?
OSCAR: I carefully organize your chaotic, meaningless lives.
DANIEL: In order for you to make a profit.
OSCAR: Meticulously organize your careless thoughts, beliefs, and lies . . . so they can have a dramatic action.
DANIEL: Really?
OSCAR: A purpose.
DANIEL: So without you our lives have no purpose?

OSCAR: You said that, not me.

DANIEL: You play with us.

OSCAR: Really?

DANIEL: Now you are going to play with him.

OSCAR: I was not playing. I care about him.

DANIEL: Him or his story? New fuel for your novels.

OSCAR: Should I drink his blood?

DANIEL: He is cute.

OSCAR: He is more than cute.

DANIEL: I wouldn't mind fucking him.

OSCAR: You should stop trying to pick up your cousins.

DANIEL: But you said . . . it was good to . . .

OSCAR: It will lead you nowhere, believe me.

DANIEL: Fuck off!

OSCAR: You'll see.

(Oscar goes to Ismael and begins to kiss him.)

ISMAEL: Fidel!

(Oscar starts to suck on Ismael's neck.)

ISMAEL: No, *primo!*

OSCAR: Incest is best!

ISMAEL: Step off!

(Ismael kicks Oscar away.)

Just because I fucked tourists for a sandwich does not mean
I am a faggot.

OSCAR: Yes it does.

ISMAEL: *¡Maricón de mierda!*

OSCAR: Come on, Cousin, don't you want it?! Wanna make a dollar?

ISMAEL: You don't own me! You not the boss of me! *¡Loco maricón!*

OSCAR: I am free. You see me jumping, Daniel? Jumping from the
plane!

ISMAEL: Enough, bullshit!

(Oscar takes out his penis.)

OSCAR: I can piss on the floor also. Come on, give me a picture of my dad so I can piss all over it and call it art. I can be a fucking hip hopper, just like you. Word?

DANIEL: Don't you dare piss anywhere. This is a classy place.

ISMAEL: *¡Loco! ¡Eres un loco!*

OSCAR: Sure, crazy like you. *Soy cubano.*

DANIEL: Cuban-American.

ISMAEL: American.

OSCAR: No.

ISMAEL: Yes. American.

OSCAR: You'll see.

ISMAEL: Who the hell put this suit on me?

DANIEL: Put your dick away.

OSCAR: Fine. For now.

DANIEL: Fine.

(Oscar zips up.)

ISMAEL: That only works when you are rapping. Who put this motherfucking suit on me?

OSCAR: The family.

ISMAEL: Why?

DANIEL: They do it to all of us.

OSCAR: Daniel, go inside. Tell my father to come in here. Tell him that his cousin is awake.

DANIEL: Fine.

OSCAR: Thank you.

(Daniel exits. Oscar looks through his book. He reads to Ismael.)

I don't have the courage to be a revolutionary.

ISMAEL: No. You do not.

(The door opens. Osvaldo enters. Miriam follows him.)

OSCAR: Dad, your cousin. Ismael.

OSVALDO: Jesus! *(He covers his nose with a handkerchief)*

MIRIAM: We got him a new suit.

OSVALDO: Sister, get someone to take that boy home. He needs to take a bath.

MIRIAM: Of course. Come, Ismael.

ISMAEL: Sure, Prima. Primo, I hate Fidel!

OSVALDO: Good boy.

ISMAEL: May he rot! Fidel.

(Ismael spits on the ground.)

OSVALDO: I wish you were my son.

ISMAEL: Fidel, he is the devil!

OSVALDO: We are going to get you a good job.

OSCAR: He has no skills, Papá. He is into hip hop.

OSVALDO: What?

ISMAEL: I do, I'm a hip hop thug from the streets of . . .

OSVALDO: We will have to teach you about business.

ISMAEL: Record business! Slide the vinyl.

OSVALDO: No, real business. We'll send you to computer school or something.

ISMAEL: I'm an artist.

OSVALDO: Not anymore.

ISMAEL: Why?

OSVALDO: In America you have to work for a living.

ISMAEL: Really?

OSVALDO: Yes. No hand-outs here.

ISMAEL: I thought you were all rich?

OSVALDO: We worked for it.

ISMAEL: But! I have a . . .

OSVALDO: We will figure it all out. But for now. Get rid of those dirty clothes and somebody get him to take a shower.

MIRIAM: I'll get one of our cousins to take him home.

OSVALDO: Good.

ISMAEL: Capitalism is heavy, bro.

OSCAR: It eats you up.

ISMAEL: It won't eat me up, 'cause I'm a thug!

OSCAR: You'll see.

ISMAEL: When you go to the hood. Cojímar. Let me know if you like it.

OSCAR: I will.

OSVALDO: Get him out of here, Sister.

ISMAEL: Cousin, I believe in the slang and the love of the word and the hip and the hop . . . from the streets of . . .

MIRIAM: Enough.

ISMAEL *(Rapping)*: I start to think and then I sink into the paper like I was ink. When I'm writing I'm trapped in between the lines. I escape when I finish the rhyme. Am I crossing the line?

(Miriam and Ismael exit.)

OSCAR: Papá.

OSVALDO: What?

OSCAR: Who was I?

OSVALDO: A little boy.

OSCAR: Daddy, I'm still a little boy.

OSVALDO: A happy little boy.

OSCAR: Who was he?

OSVALDO: A laughing little boy. A smart little boy. The polite son. I had a polite son . . . The beautiful eyes, the clear skin. Beauty and brains thrown away for the pursuit of what?

OSCAR: What?

OSVALDO: Self-degrading smut. How about pride, honor, duty? How about determination? How about a sense of loyalty? How about patriotism? Honoring your father and your mother. The things that you so conveniently forgot.

OSCAR: Pride?

OSVALDO: Yes.

OSCAR: You think I have no pride!

OSVALDO: Look what you've turned into.

OSCAR: What?

OSVALDO: My eternal nightmare.

OSCAR: Forgive me.

OSVALDO: Never.

OSCAR: Please, Papá, please forgive me.

(Oscar starts to cry.)

OSVALDO: No tears.

OSCAR: No tears? You want no tears.

OSVALDO: Absolutely.

OSCAR: If there are no tears, will you forgive me?

OSVALDO: You have no children.

OSCAR: I have my books.

OSVALDO: There was never a wedding at a Catholic church. A graduation at a university. A baseball game won.

OSCAR: But my books have meaning. People read them even in Australia.

OSVALDO: Sometimes people call me and they say, "Oh, Osvaldo, your son's a genius." Sometimes they call me and they say, "Poor Osvaldo, the things your son has said about you. What a horrible bastard your son is." Those books are your revenge.

OSCAR: Haven't you ever wanted to read them?

OSVALDO: No.

OSCAR: You know people criticize me for writing too much about us . . . You know why, Dad?

OSVALDO: I suppose you are going to tell me.

OSCAR: 'Cause they think we are only third class. Latinos. Immigrants whose only story is how they have succeeded in becoming Americans.

OSVALDO: We have. I made it—

OSCAR: With no complexity, no past, no pride. I fight them with my books, aren't you proud of me?

OSVALDO: I would have liked it better if you ran a car dealership.

OSCAR: Really?

OSVALDO: Absolutely.

OSCAR: You are so sure of yourself.

OSVALDO: Yes I am.

OSCAR: Just like Fidel!

OSVALDO: What?

OSCAR: You won't let go of power.

OSVALDO: Power?

OSCAR: The power you both have over me!

OSVALDO: Fidel Castro has power over you?

OSCAR: Dad, I am going to go to Cuba and I am going to kiss Fidel. Like this Dad.

(Oscar kisses Osvaldo. Osvaldo pushes him away. Miriam and Daniel enter, carrying trays of empty coffee cups.)

DANIEL: They want more café.

OSCAR: You want more, Dad?

OSVALDO: I'm your father.

OSCAR: So, Pedro was your brother.

DANIEL: I guess Cubans can't get enough café.

OSCAR: I went to the room upstairs. In Cuba . . . In the past. I worshiped you when I was a kid . . . I opened the door and I found you and Uncle Pedro . . .

OSVALDO: Not in front of them. Please.

MIRIAM: Daniel, go!

DANIEL: No.

OSCAR: You two seemed so happy . . . you told me to keep what I saw a secret . . . you were very nice to me, we all sat on the bed, Uncle got dressed then you got dressed, and we played with hand puppets, remember? Uncle Pedro had a box filled with them.

OSVALDO: Yes. I remember the puppets.

OSCAR: The puppets asked me questions, they taught me how to lie, how to keep your secret . . . I promised not to ever tell.

OSVALDO: I only remember the puppets.

OSCAR: I promised I would never tell. I loved you so much, Dad. You were my whole world. I'm sorry I did not keep my promise.

OSVALDO: I never made you promise anything.

OSCAR: That's right, it was the puppet.

DANIEL: Oh my God! Mamá!

MIRIAM: Oscar, you're such a greedy monster.

OSCAR: It comes from having nothing. It comes from living only in memory.

MIRIAM: You want to hurt us.

OSCAR: Isn't that what family is for?

OSVALDO: You have no heart.

OSCAR: It was stolen from me.

DANIEL: Mamá. Did you know!?

MIRIAM: Go, Son, this not about you, this is about Cuba. You were born here.

DANIEL: Yes I was. But. Did you know?

MIRIAM: About what?

DANIEL: My uncle's homosexuality.

OSVALDO: Do not use that word!

MIRIAM: I knew they loved each other.

DANIEL: Love?

OSCAR: Love.

MIRIAM: Yes, Oscar. Go, Daniel.

DANIEL: Cousin. Someday I will go to Cuba. I promise.

OSCAR: When it's not dangerous anymore?

DANIEL: When it's free.

(Daniel exits.)

OSCAR: You think it was love?

MIRIAM: The love in a family. It can take all sort of turns and twisted paths. You are a writer, you know I'm right.

OSVALDO: I've had enough.

(Miriam grabs Osvaldo's hand.)

MIRIAM: No, you have to stay.

(He stays.)

Tell me why I should forgive you, Oscar?

OSCAR: I have nothing to believe in anymore.

MIRIAM: Why?

OSCAR: My best friend killed herself three months ago. She was so talented. I thought her talent would save her. But it did not; in the end, talent doesn't save you. If my talent can't save me, how the fuck am I going to survive you?

MIRIAM: She was a writer like you?

OSCAR: No. She was a writer like no one else on earth.

OSVALDO: So, what!

OSCAR: I live on the eighteenth floor and I keep wanting to jump! Every knife is a way to cut myself . . . Dad? Look.

(He rolls up his sleeves. His arms are all cut.)

MIRIAM: You cut deep.

OSCAR: Did I?

MIRIAM: You weren't kidding.

OSCAR: No, I wasn't.

MIRIAM: You came close.

OSCAR: Dad?

OSVALDO: What?

OSCAR: Don't you have anything to say?

OSVALDO: You should have become a lawyer.

OSCAR: That's all you have to say?

OSVALDO: Yes.

OSCAR: Cuba will have meaning.

OSVALDO: Then go find meaning and leave me alone.

OSCAR: I've left you alone all my life. I have lived a life without any of you. But you know what. Tomorrow when I see Cuba again. I know I will forgive you.

OSVALDO: Won't make any difference to me. Good night.

(Osvaldo exits.)

MIRIAM: When you go to the house say hello for me. Say, "House, Miriam says hello."

OSCAR: When you bury her say good-bye for me. Say, "Mamá, Oscar says good-bye."

MIRIAM: When you kiss Fidel, bite his tongue for me until it bleeds. No, cut it off with your teeth. Cuba will love you.

OSCAR: Forgive me?

MIRIAM: I do.

(Oscar opens the door to the parking lot. Looks out.)

OSCAR: It's morning.

MIRIAM: Thank God, it's time to bury her. I wonder if anyone will ever forgive me.

(Oscar goes.)

I hope you get there, Oscar. See, I'm not such a bitch. See, Mamá?

(Yolanda enters.)

YOLANDA: The casket is about to be closed.

MIRIAM: Fine.

YOLANDA: You don't want to kiss her good-bye?

MIRIAM: I kissed her good-bye thirty years ago.

YOLANDA: That's true.

MIRIAM: Yes, it is.

YOLANDA: When you left me alone with Pedro.

MIRIAM: When?

YOLANDA: When you came here and I stayed.

MIRIAM: Yes.

YOLANDA: Then Osvaldo and my sister left.

MIRIAM: I remember.

YOLANDA: Osvaldo asked me to protect his parents from Pedro. Remember, he was such a mean drunk?

MIRIAM: Who wasn't?

YOLANDA: I understood Pedro . . . we were the only ones left of our group, our generation . . . I would drive from bar to bar . . . at night . . . I would eventually find him. Sometimes he was beat up . . . sometimes . . . I'd have to find a man that would carry him to my car . . . I would drive him to your house. Drag him into his room. I would undress him . . . clean him with a damp cloth . . . sometimes there were burn marks on his body, cigarettes I think . . . sometimes there was blood. Poor thing.

MIRIAM: What a wasted life.

(Miriam starts to laugh.)

YOLANDA: Miriam, you can't laugh at your mother's funeral.

MIRIAM: This is not our real life, right?

YOLANDA: Miami?

MIRIAM: Yes.

YOLANDA: I hope not.

MIRIAM: Good, because in my real life I want to be a faithful wife.

YOLANDA: You're a good woman.

MIRIAM: In whose eyes?

YOLANDA: Mine.

MIRIAM: The only eyes that count, right?

YOLANDA: That's right, because I stayed behind and suffered.

MIRIAM: Yes, Yolanda, you stayed and you suffered and you paid for our sins.

YOLANDA: I did.

MIRIAM: You don't think I suffered, too, here in Miami? You know I had this nightmare every night that I cut Fidel's balls off . . .

YOLANDA: How often?

MIRIAM: Every night for the last thirty years . . . I cut them off . . . I put them in a glass jar and buried them in the sand in front of "La Terraza." Then I go in and order a mojito . . . And drink every last drop . . . and looked out on the beach . . . Cojímar. Our Cojímar . . . and I watch them float out to sea . . . *(She laughs)* My God, Yolanda, I'm crying. *(Laughing and crying)* Mamá, I'm crying.

(They both laugh and cry.)

YOLANDA: Finally.

MIRIAM: Yes.

YOLANDA: You've gone home.

MIRIAM: I have. Yes, I've gone home. Let's go bury her.

YOLANDA: But not the past. Never the past.

MIRIAM: No, we will never forget what Fidel did to us.

YOLANDA: Good.

MIRIAM: Get the shovel. I want to bury her myself.

    (Miriam and Yolanda laugh.
       Blackout.)

END OF PLAY

THE COOK

For Amy Madigan

The Cook was originally commissioned by the Cherry Lane Theatre (Angelina Fiordellisi, Artistic Director) and premiered in December 2003 at INTAR Hispanic Arts Center in New York City (Max Ferrá, Founder and Producing Artistic Director). The production was directed by Michael John Garcés; the set design was by Antje Ellermann, the costume design was by Elizabeth Hope Clancy, the lighting design was by Kirk Bookman, the sound design was by David M. Lawson and the original music was by José Conde. It was performed by:

GLADYS	Zabryna Guevara
CARLOS	Jason Madera
ELENA/ROSA	Nilaja Sun
ADRIA/LOURDES	Maggie Bofill
JULIO	Jason Quarles

The final draft of *The Cook* (which is printed here) premiered in November 2007 at Seattle Repertory Theatre (David Esbjornson, Artistic Director; Benjamin Moore, Managing Director). It was directed by Juliette Carrillo; the set design was by Mikiko Suzuki MacAdams, the costume design was by Elizabeth Hope Clancy, the lighting design was by Geoff Korf and the music composition/sound design was by Chris Webb. The stage manager was Amy Poisson and the assistant stage manager was Lori Amondson Flint. It was performed by:

GLADYS	Zabryna Guevara
CARLOS	Al Espinosa
ELENA/ROSA	Jessica Pimentel
ADRIA/LOURDES	Yetta Gottesman
JULIO	A.K. Murtadha

Characters

GLADYS

CARLOS

ELENA

ADRIA

JULIO

ROSA

LOURDES

Time and Place

El Vedado, a district of La Habana, Cuba
Act I: New Year's Eve, 1958
Act II: 1972
Act III: 1997

ACT ONE

A mansion in El Vedado, a district of La Habana, Cuba. December 31, 1958.
Gladys, the cook, is talking to her husband, Carlos, the chauffeur. They are
both in their early thirties. They are in the kitchen. The kitchen is luxurious.
They are in the middle of serving a New Year's Eve party. There is a big
bucket of homemade ice cream on top of a counter. Carlos is trying to steal a
taste with a spoon. Gladys is brushing his hand away.

GLADYS: No, Carlos!
CARLOS: Just a little bit, baby. Just a little taste of something sweet
    on my lips.
GLADYS: Kiss me then.
CARLOS: Come on.
GLADYS: My lips are sweeter than any dessert.
CARLOS: Baby! A taste, that's all.
GLADYS: It's for the party!
CARLOS: They won't know.
GLADYS: But I will.
CARLOS: They're all drunk. Who cares.
GLADYS: I care.
CARLOS: Come on, one taste.

GLADYS: I said no.

CARLOS: Oh, really.

GLADYS: Yes.

CARLOS: Are you going to tell me what to do?

GLADYS: That's right.

CARLOS: It's New Year's Eve. Something's gotta be for me.

GLADYS: I don't mix business with pleasure.

CARLOS: They won't mind.

GLADYS: But I mind. It's my job. What if we run out?

CARLOS: Are you kidding?

GLADYS: We work for them.

CARLOS: So?

GLADYS: So we don't eat their food. Unless they tell us to.

CARLOS: I'm having some and that's that.

(He takes a little spoonful.)

GLADYS: You'll never learn.

CARLOS: This is good! This is goddamned delicious!

GLADYS: Really?

CARLOS: Baby.

GLADYS: I am your baby.

CARLOS: What a cook!

GLADYS: Well.

CARLOS: What fruit did you put in it?

GLADYS: Guess.

CARLOS: I gotta take another bite.

GLADYS: Nothing like homemade ice cream.

CARLOS: Another taste, please.

GLADYS: Use another spoon.

CARLOS: Why?

GLADYS: That one has your saliva on it.

CARLOS: Jesus!

(She gives him another spoon.)

GLADYS: Don't complain, you're getting another bite.

(Carlos takes the other spoon.)

Taste it.

(He does.)

CARLOS: Mango?
GLADYS: No.
CARLOS: Papaya?
GLADYS: Way off.
CARLOS: Guayaba, has to be guayaba.
GLADYS: Guayaba? For the Señora Adria Santana? Are you kidding?
CARLOS: How do I know?
GLADYS: She has a more delicate palate.
CARLOS: Really? Well . . . Well . . .
GLADYS: It's strawberry.
CARLOS: Hmm. Strawberry.
GLADYS: Do you like it better than the lime?
CARLOS: Better than the lime?
GLADYS: Yes, do you? You had the lime last year. Bring in '58 with lime, '59 with strawberry.
CARLOS: And '60 with rum?
GLADYS: I don't know about the future.
CARLOS: I do.
GLADYS: I don't want to hear about it.
CARLOS: You're gonna have to . . .

(Elena enters.)

ELENA: It's fun.
GLADYS: Elena. You're so sweet.

(Elena exits.)

CARLOS: Give me another spoonful.

(Gladys laughs.)

GLADYS: When it's finished.

CARLOS: It's delicious. It has to be finished.

GLADYS: No! Now it's going to turn into "Baked Alaska"!

CARLOS: What?

GLADYS: Cake underneath, meringue on top. Then right before the New Year, I put it in the oven to brown.

CARLOS: Are you crazy?

GLADYS: No.

CARLOS: It will melt!

GLADYS: Apparently not.

CARLOS: Impossible.

GLADYS: Señora Adria had it in New York.

CARLOS: Another American invention.

GLADYS: Yes, apparently their ice cream does not melt. And their shit does not stink, and they don't overthrow their leaders with revolutions.

CARLOS: See? You talked about it.

GLADYS: You tricked me.

CARLOS: You know what's going on.

GLADYS: Maybe.

CARLOS: I'm sure of it. We're going to get rid of all the fucking foreigners that are trying to control our country. When I was at the Union Hall, they said it was only days away . . . that Batista's army was going to turn around and . . .

GLADYS: I don't want to know.

(We hear a bell ring.)

They need more hors d'oeuvres. Go.

CARLOS: I'm the chauffeur, not a waiter.

GLADYS: It's a big party.

(The bell rings again.)

Pick up the tray and stop bullshitting.

CARLOS: Didn't you hire two of your cousins?

GLADYS: They needed the work.

CARLOS: Why can't they take the trays of hors d'oeuvres?

GLADYS: They're out there working. You are the one that is in here eating.

CARLOS: If someone wants me to drive them somewhere, I will.

GLADYS: It's the first time they're trying to serve at a big classy party. Please, I need you to help them . . .

CARLOS: Serve?

GLADYS: Yes!

CARLOS: Obviously your cousins are just a bunch of . . .

GLADYS: Go. Help them. Before you say my cousins are lazy niggers!

CARLOS: Well . . .

GLADYS: You're not that white!

CARLOS: Café?

GLADYS: Really? Well!

CARLOS: Café, my skin is the color of café with . . .

GLADYS: Very little milk.

CARLOS: And you're what? A drop of espresso in a cup full of milk?

GLADYS: I know who I am.

CARLOS: Really?

GLADYS: Absolutely.

CARLOS: A lady in waiting. To the great Adria. Pure white milk, descended from Spain. Adria Santana.

GLADYS: No. I'm not a lady in waiting.

CARLOS: I'm surprised you don't want the title.

GLADYS: I'm a great cook.

CARLOS: So?

GLADYS: That's who I am. Take the tray and work.

(She hands him the tray. Carlos admires the hors d'oeuvres.)

CARLOS: Beautiful.

GLADYS: See? I can cook.

CARLOS: You should be working at a fancy hotel.

GLADYS: At hotels, cooks are men.

CARLOS: Come the revolution . . .

GLADYS: Cooks at hotels will still be men.

CARLOS: You're wrong.

GLADYS: I like it here. I like where I am.

CARLOS: Funny, I thought you were waiting for the revolution, just like I am.

GLADYS: Well, I am not . . .

CARLOS: Why not?

GLADYS: They don't like it.

CARLOS: Your masters?

GLADYS: The people we work for.

CARLOS: Well, the people you work for have helped turn our country into a floating casino. They have made us dependent on the U.S. dollars and the U.S. tourists—and all they want is a little bit of pussy and a place where they can gamble, drink and piss. Piss all over us.

GLADYS: Shut up!

CARLOS: Fidel Castro's revolution will give power and dignity back to the people of Cuba.

GLADYS: Jesus, Carlos, the ballroom is filled with Batista's people.

CARLOS: Second-tier Batista people.

GLADYS: Second-tier for sure. But still powerful enough to have you killed.

CARLOS: Fidel Castro's revolution. Repeat it. Revolution. Fidel Castro. Come on, get used to it. Revolution.

GLADYS: Stop it!

(The bell rings again.)

CARLOS: They're not patient either.

GLADYS: Please!

CARLOS: What, sweetie?

GLADYS: Serve them.

CARLOS: Meat pies, my favorites.

GLADYS: They're stuffed with crab.

CARLOS: Something else from the U.S.A.?

GLADYS: No. My recipe. Cuban.

(Carlos picks up one of the crab pies.)

156

CARLOS: Then I want to swallow it whole.

(He swallows the puff pastry.)

Tastes like you.

(The bell rings.)

GLADYS: Yes?
CARLOS: Salty, yet sweet.
GLADYS: Cuban, like I said.
CARLOS: Yes.

(He starts to kiss her.)

GLADYS: Honey, please, go.

(Carlos leaves. Gladys looks through a cookbook.)

(Reading): "Preheat the oven to four hundred and fifty degrees."

(She goes and lights the oven. She continues reading the cookbook.)

"Cut the cake into one-inch squares. Put the squares on a cookie tray. Place the ice cream on top, but make sure it's hard." *(To herself)* It's so hard I can't scoop it out yet. *(Reading)* "Cover it with meringue. Then put it in the oven till the meringue is golden. Serve it immediately." *(To herself)* This is not going to be easy. Baked Alaska for fifty, maybe sixty?

(Adria has walked in during this last speech. She is in her late thirties, elegant. She is wearing an evening gown and noticeable rubies in her ears and around her neck.)

ADRIA: Who knows?
GLADYS: I've sent a cousin to count the guests. All right, next, whip the meringue and make it firm, like "The Snows of Kilimanjaro."

ADRIA: So you did read the book I gave you.

GLADYS: Yes, I love Hemingway. What a mind!

ADRIA: Yes. He's a drunk, you know. You can always see him drinking in every bar in town. But he's a great writer. Maybe he's a tortured soul. Maybe that's why he drinks. Maybe that's why he writes. Who knows? One day, the booze will destroy his brain and the rest of him, so he won't be able to write anymore.

GLADYS: I hope not. I love his stories.

ADRIA: Why?

GLADYS: He love us. He loves La Habana.

ADRIA: Yes, well, what's here not to love?

GLADYS: Nothing.

ADRIA: What time is it now?

GLADYS: Twenty-five to twelve.

(Pause.)

ADRIA: You like the new cookbook by Nitza Villapol?

GLADYS: It's as good as her television show.

ADRIA: I'm sure you're a much better cook.

GLADYS: Señora! How could that be?

ADRIA: You're really good.

GLADYS: But Nitza's on television. Women all over this country watch her.

ADRIA: Yes?

GLADYS: And worship her.

ADRIA: So?

GLADYS: So?

ADRIA: You're better.

GLADYS: Well, thank you.

ADRIA: We should send you to Paris, to a French cooking school, then you'd show them how gifted you really are.

GLADYS: I'm not.

ADRIA: Believe me. I know.

GLADYS: Really?

ADRIA: I've been to Paris.

GLADYS: I remember.

ADRIA: I had a meal in the most expensive restaurant in Paris. And I told my mother, "Gladys is better."

GLADYS: She agreed?

ADRIA: She said, "Imagine if she knew these recipes. There would be no stopping her. You'd lose her."

GLADYS: Never.

ADRIA: I'm a very lucky woman to have someone like you cooking for me.

GLADYS: All right. Flatter me. It's the holidays.

ADRIA: No, not flattery. Facts. Put the ice cream away, or it'll get too soft.

GLADYS: But I need to be able to scoop it out. It's like a rock now.

ADRIA: We have plenty of time.

GLADYS: But . . .

ADRIA: Everything is going to happen a little bit later.

GLADYS: What do you mean?

ADRIA: We need to play with time.

GLADYS: New Year's is at midnight no matter what.

ADRIA: Not this year! Ask Carlos to set the clocks back an hour. Mr. Santana is not here yet, and I cannot greet the New Year without him.

GLADYS: But . . .

ADRIA: Those bitches out there would start saying that he has a mistress—and he doesn't have a mistress.

GLADYS: Of course not.

ADRIA: Maybe their husbands need something somewhere else.

GLADYS: Maybe.

ADRIA: I mean, look at them, so tight . . .

GLADYS: Yes.

ADRIA: Or overly voluptuous.

GLADYS: Fat.

ADRIA: They don't walk enough.

GLADYS: You think?

ADRIA: They don't fuck enough.

GLADYS: You're sure?

ADRIA: Too many bonbons instead of cocks.

GLADYS: Religious girls.

ADRIA: The worst kind.

GLADYS: Yes.

ADRIA: That's for damn sure.

GLADYS: Jesus, forgive us.

ADRIA: There's enough woman in me for twenty men. My husband, he knows it. He worships me. My skin, my eyes, my breasts, my hips, my ass.

GLADYS: You are beautiful.

ADRIA: So are you.

GLADYS: Thank you.

ADRIA: I mean it.

GLADYS: I appreciate it.

ADRIA: If it wasn't for the fact that you work for me, we could be friends.

GLADYS: I feel we are.

ADRIA: My mother thinks it's cruel to be friends with people that work for you.

(Pause.)

GLADYS: We're a certain kind of friends.

ADRIA: What kind?

GLADYS: Someone who's always there, next to you. Nothing has to be said.

ADRIA: Yes.

GLADYS: Nothing has to be said.

ADRIA: But I want to.

GLADYS: Fine.

ADRIA: I have a great affection towards you.

GLADYS: The feeling is mutual, Señora.

(They embrace.)

ADRIA: Oh.

GLADYS: Señora.

(Adria lets out a scream.)

ADRIA: Ay! Ay!

GLADYS: What's wrong? Señora.

ADRIA: Sometimes when a victim is being strangled, she lets out a
scream.

GLADYS: Tell me who's strangling you.

ADRIA: Fidel Castro!

(Pause.)

GLADYS: Oh.

ADRIA: You understand?

GLADYS: I'm trying.

ADRIA: The bastard.

GLADYS: Things look bad?

ADRIA: Maybe.

GLADYS: You can trust me.

(Adria looks at Gladys.)

ADRIA: Can I?

GLADYS: Yes.

ADRIA: No matter what.

GLADYS: Yes.

ADRIA: I want to. I want to tell you.

GLADYS: I want to hear it.

(Adria starts to cry.)

You're crying.

ADRIA: Yes, things are bad. Disaster.

GLADYS: I could feel it.

ADRIA: And the tragedy is I could be happy if it wasn't for that
bastard and his goddamned revolution. Gladys, I'm pregnant!

GLADYS: Finally!

ADRIA: Just when I thought it was all going to go away.

GLADYS: I knew it would happen.

ADRIA: I'll be able to lie about my age.

GLADYS: Yes!

ADRIA: With a baby in my arms, they'll believe I'm just thirty.

GLADYS: Good.

ADRIA: Yes. But the father does nothing but worry. Worry about his future. His money. His life.

GLADYS: The baby didn't make him happy? He's been waiting for twelve years.

ADRIA: I haven't told him.

GLADYS: Oh.

ADRIA: I wanted to be sure.

GLADYS: Of course.

ADRIA: But I'm going to tell him tonight.

GLADYS: The situation will change.

ADRIA: Yes.

GLADYS: Feel better.

ADRIA: I do.

GLADYS: Good.

ADRIA: Yes, let's start with your watch.

GLADYS: Why not?

(Gladys gives Adria her watch.)

ADRIA: Nice.

GLADYS: You know Carlos.

ADRIA: It reads 11:40, but ... Puff! Magic ... and it's 10:40. And now, mine. Your husband can do the rest.

(Julio enters.)

JULIO: Seventy-two guests.

(Julio exits.)

ADRIA: Do we have enough hors d'oeuvres?

GLADYS: Of course.

ADRIA: What a silly question.

GLADYS: You know me.

ADRIA: Always making double than what's needed.

GLADYS: My crime.

ADRIA: Yes, we'll keep feeding them. Keep those hypocritical sons of bitches happy.

(Carlos enters.)

Carlos, please, my husband is going to be late.

CARLOS: Yes?

ADRIA: So New Year's is going to have to be later.

CARLOS: How?

GLADYS: Set the clocks back an hour.

CARLOS: What?

GLADYS: That's right.

ADRIA: Yes. Set the clocks back an hour. Our's are.

(She shows him her watch.)

It's an hour earlier.

CARLOS: But.

ADRIA: By my watch, in my house.

CARLOS: But . . .

ADRIA: It's what I've decided.

CARLOS: Who's going to believe . . . ?

GLADYS: It's what she needs you to do.

CARLOS: And you agree with her?

GLADYS: Yes.

CARLOS: But . . .

ADRIA: That's what I want at my party.

GLADYS: That's what she wants.

CARLOS: Fine.

ADRIA: Do it in a way that they don't notice.

CARLOS: Sure!

ADRIA: Good.

GLADYS: Settled.

ADRIA: Yes.

GLADYS: Easy.

ADRIA: It is.

GLADYS: So, stop worrying.

CARLOS: How about their watches?

ADRIA: We didn't think of that.

GLADYS: They'll think they're fast.

ADRIA: Yes. Right.

CARLOS: Whatever you say.

ADRIA: Start with the big one in the hallway. Gladys, the ice cream—in the freezer!

GLADYS: It's in there already.

ADRIA: Good.

(Adria leaves.)

GLADYS: Go change the clocks.

CARLOS: Sometimes I look at all this and wonder why it's not mine.

GLADYS: Fate.

CARLOS: Or the color of my skin.

GLADYS: So now you're black.

CARLOS: To them. Or maybe it's that I was born poor.

GLADYS: Jesus loves the poor more than the rich.

CARLOS: Really?

GLADYS: Don't get bitter. Go and change the clocks.

CARLOS: Playing with time.

GLADYS: Yes. We are. She said if I didn't work for her we could be friends.

CARLOS: And that made you feel good?

GLADYS: Yes, warm.

CARLOS: I want more.

GLADYS: That could be dangerous.

CARLOS: Don't worry about me. I'm gonna win.

GLADYS: That would be nice.

CARLOS: And I'll buy you a restaurant.

GLADYS: What for? You're going to get rid of the tourists.

CARLOS: Cubans will still eat out.

GLADYS: Dreamer.

CARLOS: But that's what you love about me.

GLADYS: That's what I love and what scares me.

(She kisses him.)

CARLOS: Nice. So do I really have to change the clocks?
GLADYS: If you want another kiss. Go. She's gonna ring the bell if you don't do it soon . . .

(The bell rings.)

See? Send in one of my cousins. I need help. I have to make more hors d'oeuvres.
CARLOS: So you don't have it all under control.
GLADYS: I will.

(Carlos exits. Elena enters.)

Time changes. Time is always moving. The cookbook is always the same. But if you improvise on the recipe in the slightest way, it changes, it becomes a whole new dish.
ELENA: Beautiful.

(Gladys grabs her cookbook and sits in a chair. Elena exits.)

GLADYS: "To cook in a minute." Nitza, help me. Save me. I need your minute. Right now, today, when a minute is everything. Should I look under breads and muffins? Or sandwiches and petit sandwiches? Petite sandwiches, on page three hundred and one. Stuffed eggs? No, that's for a day on the beach, not New Year's.

(Julio, Gladys's cousin, walks in. He is very dark, lean and beautiful. He is twenty.)

JULIO: You need me?
GLADYS: What?
JULIO: Carlos said you needed me.

GLADYS: He did?

JULIO: Yes.

GLADYS: I do.

JULIO: Well, here I am.

GLADYS: I'm going to make finger sandwiches.

JULIO: What kind?

GLADYS: I haven't decided yet.

JULIO: Oh. I think . . .

GLADYS: Take off the crust.

JULIO: I know how.

GLADYS: Good.

JULIO: I like being with you in the kitchen.

GLADYS: In the drawer. The bread knife.

JULIO: Sure.

GLADYS: The drawer on the left.

JULIO: I'm opening it.

GLADYS: You know what it looks like?

JULIO: What?

GLADYS: The knife.

JULIO: Well, I think . . .

GLADYS: Very long and very flat.

JULIO: That's right. Very long and very flat.

(Julio opens the drawer.)

GLADYS: I've decided!

JULIO: What's it going to be?

GLADYS: I'll make a spread with cream cheese and pimento and another one with anchovies.

(Julio starts to slice the bread. Gladys starts getting cream cheese and the other ingredients and makes the spread. She starts humming a song. Julio starts doing some dance steps.)

Dancing while you work.

JULIO: As long as you get the work done.

GLADYS: True.

(Gladys hums along and does a couple of steps.)

How long has it been since I've gone to a dance on New Year's?

JULIO: Pity.

GLADYS: That's what happens when you work for a living.

(Elena enters.)

JULIO: Are you running out of food?

GLADYS: We might.

JULIO: It's almost midnight.

GLADYS: At this house, New Year's is going to take longer than you think.

JULIO: Oh.

ELENA: Sure. *(Pause)* Good.

(Elena exits.)

GLADYS: High society. Or is it odd society?

JULIO: I like it. The men in their white tuxedos. They look beautiful, don't you think?

GLADYS: This is a classy crowd.

JULIO: La Habana is one of the few places where you can wear white at New Year's.

GLADYS: Even the women.

JULIO: In the rest of the world it's black.

GLADYS: You like fashion?

JULIO: Yes.

GLADYS: I see.

JULIO: So?

GLADYS: Nothing.

JULIO: Good. Nothing wrong with liking fashion.

GLADYS: Nothing.

JULIO: I'm glad you feel that way.

GLADYS: I'm not backwards.

JULIO: I know.

GLADYS: Good.

JULIO: I might want to be a hairdresser.

GLADYS: You mean a barber?

JULIO: No, when it's for women, it's called a hairdresser or a coiffeur.

GLADYS: Want to be near the ladies, huh? You are a sly one.

JULIO: For sure!

GLADYS: How's your girlfriend?

JULIO: She left me.

GLADYS: I'm sorry.

JULIO: I'm young.

GLADYS: Are you heartbroken?

JULIO: We had a split, that's all.

GLADYS: Well.

JULIO: Your bread is sliced.

GLADYS: The spread is ready. Here we go!

JULIO: You want me to help you spread it?

GLADYS: Men are not good at doing things like this.

JULIO: Maybe.

GLADYS: Not really.

(Gladys spreads the paste.)

JULIO: You want me to make the anchovy spread?

GLADYS: I'm the cook.

JULIO: In great restaurants, cooks are men.

GLADYS: Not in this one!

JULIO: Of course not.

GLADYS: Beautiful, huh?

(Gladys arranges sandwiches in a tray. Julio looks at his watch.)

JULIO: Fifteen minutes till 1959.

GLADYS: An hour and fifteen minutes!

JULIO: No. My watch is right. It runs perfectly.

GLADYS: This house is on a different time.

JULIO: What?

GLADYS: We set all the clocks back an hour.

(The bell rings.)

Oh God! She needs the hors d'oeuvres!

(Gladys starts to cry.)

JULIO: Don't cry.
GLADYS: Tonight, I think tonight the world is going to turn inside
  out!
JULIO: I see.
GLADYS: Do you?
JULIO: I listen to the news.
GLADYS: We all do.
JULIO: We all hear everything and then pretend we didn't hear it.
GLADYS: It's only human.
JULIO: Yes.

(Pause.)

GLADYS: I gotta work.
JULIO: Please let me help you.
GLADYS: There is no other choice.
JULIO: I'll do a good job. I promise.
GLADYS: I know you will, Julio.

(The bell rings. Elena enters.)

ELENA: This is hard!

(Elena exits.)

GLADYS: Chop the anchovies real fine.
JULIO: Done!
GLADYS: I'll arrange another tray.

(She starts to work. The phone rings. She answers it, but continues to work.)

Santana's . . . Oh Señor . . . Yes, we are waiting for you. She's in the party. I'm in the kitchen. New Year's is waiting for you . . . How? We set the clocks back . . . *(She laughs)* Yes, her idea of course . . . An hour . . . Believe me, it's not going to happen till you get here . . . We do have our ways . . . Oh, Señora Adria . . . Yes! Yes, Señora . . . Excuse me.

(Carlos walks in with an empty tray.)

CARLOS: No one is falling for the time change.
GLADYS: We got to keep them eating.
JULIO: "Let them eat cake!"
GLADYS: Not yet.
JULIO: No, that's what Marie Antoinette said.
CARLOS: Who?
JULIO: She was the Queen of France when the revolutionaries were at the door.
GLADYS: There are no revolutionaries at the door.

(Gladys starts to work.)

CARLOS: How do you know this stuff?
JULIO: I go to the movies.
CARLOS: Too much of the time, if you ask me.
JULIO: I didn't ask you.
GLADYS: Carlos, fill the tray with those sandwiches. Julio, spread more paste on another loaf. I'll cut them. I have to make sure they look right on the tray. The way something looks is everything!
CARLOS: Nothing like a woman's touch.
GLADYS: Really?
CARLOS: Really.
GLADYS: Thank you.
CARLOS: I know you're nervous, but remember that I love you.
GLADYS: No matter what changes?

CARLOS: Change is good.

GLADYS: Go serve the sandwiches, please.

(Carlos eats one.)

CARLOS: Delicious.

GLADYS: Don't eat anymore!

CARLOS: I'm your taster.

GLADYS: Go.

CARLOS: I will, this time without a fight.

(Carlos goes.)

JULIO: I'm going to make more.

GLADYS: Good.

JULIO: I did a good job with the last ones.

GLADYS: Yes, you did, Julio. A very good job. I'll get another tray.

JULIO: They sure can eat, the ruling class.

GLADYS: So can the working class.

JULIO: Yeah.

(Gladys gets a tray and puts doilies on it.)

Chic.

GLADYS: Yes, aren't they?

JULIO: For sure.

GLADYS: Not too old fashioned?

JULIO: No.

(They start setting sandwiches on the tray.)

How long have you been working here?

GLADYS: In this house?

JULIO: Yes.

GLADYS: Twelve years.

JULIO: Long time.

GLADYS: Maybe.

JULIO: Seems like a long time to me.

GLADYS: I came over to this house when Adria got married. I started working for her family when I was thirteen. I started doing the laundry, ironing simple things. Then I showed a talent for cooking and Señora Santana's mother encouraged it. She is responsible for my vocation.

JULIO: And you're grateful.

GLADYS: Grateful? No.

JULIO: All right.

GLADYS: Indebted.

(Adria is there. She is wearing a black mink coat and carries a beach bag.)

JULIO: My God! What a vision!

ADRIA: What's your name?

JULIO: Julio Gomez.

GLADYS: He's my cousin.

JULIO: Yes, I am.

ADRIA: Good.

JULIO: I handed you a drink earlier this evening.

ADRIA: I don't remember.

JULIO: You were very nice to me.

ADRIA: So, you can be trusted.

JULIO: Absolutely.

ADRIA: Gladys, can he be?

JULIO: I can.

GLADYS: Yes, he can be.

ADRIA: Good.

JULIO: Yes.

ADRIA: Come closer.

JULIO: Can I touch it.

GLADYS: Señora.

ADRIA: What?

JULIO: The mink coat.

ADRIA: Yes, you can.

JULIO: Black mink! Sweet Jesus!

(Julio stands by her and touches the coat.)

I've only seen pictures of it in *Vogue.*
GLADYS: You've touched enough.
ADRIA: Hold my hand.
JULIO: What?
GLADYS: Just do it, Julio.
JULIO: Fine.

(Julio holds her hand.)

You're shaking.
GLADYS: You are?
ADRIA: That doesn't matter.
JULIO: Are you sure?
ADRIA: Listen to me!
GLADYS: Listen to her!
JULIO: I am! Jesus!
GLADYS: Don't get so uppity.
JULIO: I'm not.
ADRIA: Just listen.
GLADYS: We are.

(They look at Adria.)

ADRIA: Quietly go up to Carlos. Tell him to bring the car to the back
    alley. He should wait for me there. You're not to say anything to
    anyone. Either one of you.
JULIO: Yes.
ADRIA: Then continue to hand out the sandwiches.
JULIO: Fine.
GLADYS: Don't you say anything to anyone!
JULIO: I won't.
GLADYS: Take the tray!
JULIO: I will!

(He takes the tray.)

GLADYS: Everything is under control.

JULIO: What a mysterious night.

(Julio exits.)

GLADYS: Is it?

ADRIA: Mysterious?

GLADYS: Yes.

ADRIA: No.

GLADYS: No?

ADRIA: Just factual.

GLADYS: I see. Why are you wearing that coat?

ADRIA: A cold reality has entered the room.

GLADYS: What is it?

ADRIA: What? The material? Didn't you hear your cousin? Mink. It's made out of hundreds of minks. Minks are little furry rat-like animals.

GLADYS: No. The cold reality.

ADRIA: Mink. Black mink.

GLADYS: I never saw it before.

ADRIA: Reality?

GLADYS: The coat.

ADRIA: I bought it in New York.

GLADYS: Is that where you are going?

ADRIA: I don't know.

GLADYS: Please, you can trust me.

ADRIA: I do. I have to.

GLADYS: Has your mother left also?

ADRIA: My mother is vacationing in Barcelona.

GLADYS: I see.

ADRIA: I don't know where I am going, that's why I'm shaking. Can't you see me shake?

GLADYS: Yes! And it breaks my heart.

ADRIA: Oh God! Oh God! I'm scared! Oh God! Jesus! Happy New Year, you bastard. Son of a bitch, Fidel! Help me, Saint Christopher!

GLADYS: I'm sorry.

ADRIA: I do not know where I am going. All I know is I have to leave.

GLADYS: But you know it will be cold.

ADRIA: Yes.

GLADYS: Adria! My Adria! My darling Adria! What's going on?

ADRIA: Chaos.

GLADYS: Is Fidel here?

ADRIA: I imagine he is not in La Habana yet. But he is on his way.

GLADYS: I see.

ADRIA: But my husband called me. I don't know . . . He called me, told me we must leave.

GLADYS: Say good-bye to your husband for me.

ADRIA: All I know is that Batista has told us to leave. Fidel will march into La Habana tomorrow.

GLADYS: I'm so sorry.

ADRIA: You don't care about me.

GLADYS: I do.

ADRIA: How can you? You work for me.

GLADYS: I do, with all my heart, Adria . . .

ADRIA: You never called me Adria.

GLADYS: You're leaving and I want to say your name, Adria. Adria. Ah!

ADRIA: Do not let them in here.

GLADYS: I won't.

ADRIA: Fidel's army.

GLADYS: Never.

ADRIA: Fidel's people.

GLADYS: Not while I'm alive. I promise.

ADRIA: Swear it to me!

GLADYS: Over my dead body.

ADRIA: Really?

GLADYS: Trust me.

ADRIA: Maybe you want this revolution.

GLADYS: Never.

ADRIA: How can I believe you?

GLADYS: I love my life.

ADRIA: You seem to.

GLADYS: I love my life with you.

ADRIA: Thank you.

(Adria goes into her beach bag.)

I hope your cousin is doing his duty . . .

(Gladys looks out the door.)

GLADYS: He is. He's serving sandwiches.

ADRIA: Here's five hundred dollars for next month's expenses. Pay the cleaning women. If they ask where I am, say we went on a second honeymoon.

GLADYS: Second honeymoon, in Paris.

ADRIA: Yes, Paris. I like that.

GLADYS: I thought you would.

ADRIA: Second honeymoon, because I am finally pregnant. Tell them I am pregnant.

GLADYS: I'll tell the whole block.

ADRIA: Good. I'll be pregnant in the city of my dreams, Paris.

GLADYS: Wonderful.

ADRIA: So, take five. No, six. You have to pay your cousins.

GLADYS: I'm going to start crying.

ADRIA: You can't.

GLADYS: You'll be back in a month.

ADRIA: I will believe you love me, if you protect my home. If you keep it intact.

GLADYS: I will.

ADRIA: For as long as I'm gone.

GLADYS: Not an ashtray out of place. I promise.

ADRIA: Swear by the Virgin Mary.

GLADYS: I swear.

(We hear laughter and "Happy New Year!")

We couldn't fool them.

ADRIA: The New Year has come. Even in this house where we played with time.

GLADYS: A kiss good-bye.

ADRIA: Yes.

(Adria kisses Gladys on both cheeks.)

Tell them I went to Paris. Not Barcelona.

(Adria leaves.)

GLADYS: See you in a month. I'll study the cookbooks. I'll learn to make something that's popular in Paris.

(She goes to a drawer, gets a cigarillo and lights it.)

Happy New Year? Happy New Year.

(Julio walks in.)

JULIO: You're smoking.

GLADYS: I am in charge of the house.

JULIO: What?

GLADYS: She put me in charge of the house till she comes back. That's how much she trusts me.

JULIO: She's gone?

GLADYS: You want one?

JULIO: Sure.

GLADYS: Here. Let's smoke!

(They smoke.)

JULIO: Where has she gone?

GLADYS: She went to Paris.

JULIO: Really?

GLADYS: Second honeymoon. She's pregnant.

JULIO: They're asking for dessert.

GLADYS: Who?

JULIO: The guests. The people in the party.

GLADYS: I don't care.

JULIO: You don't care?

GLADYS: I don't like Adria's friends.

JULIO: You don't?

GLADYS: She didn't like them either.

(The bell rings.)

JULIO: They're hungry.

GLADYS: Tell them their world ended at midnight. Like Cinderella.

JULIO: Fidel won!

GLADYS: Yes.

JULIO: Hallelujah!

GLADYS: You're glad?

JULIO: Yes!

GLADYS: Really, Julio?

JULIO: Of course. And you, Gladys?

GLADYS: I don't know.

JULIO: I guess you'll find out.

(The bell rings.)

They are calling for dessert.

GLADYS: What shall we do?

JULIO: Keep smoking?

GLADYS: Why not?

JULIO: The revolution has come.

GLADYS: This part of the revolution, I like.

(The bell rings over and over.)

JULIO: Aggressive.

GLADYS: Yes.

JULIO: The ruling class is like that.

GLADYS: I know.

JULIO: They are going to keep calling for dessert all night.

(Elena enters.)

ELENA: They're mad.

(Gladys takes the cake pan for the Baked Alaska, hands it to Julio.)

GLADYS: Let them eat cake.
JULIO: Good.
ELENA: What?
GLADYS: Tell them that the "Baked Alaska" has melted.

(Blackout.)

ACT TWO

El Vedado, Cuba, 1972. The same kitchen. It looks exactly the same, but time has passed. It is a hot, bright summer day. Gladys is there. She is in her forties. She is dressed in a summer dress that once belonged to Adria. Julio, her cousin, is talking to her. He is now in his late thirties. He is wearing bell-bottoms, sandals and a T-shirt. He has an Afro. Gladys is making tamales.

GLADYS: So how did you know I was making tamales?
JULIO: There is always something good cooking at this house.

(He looks out the window.)

    Jesus!
GLADYS: What?
JULIO: Shut the window.
GLADYS: It's hot.
JULIO: Close the shutters.
GLADYS: No.
JULIO: Please.
GLADYS: My eyes aren't as good as they used to be.
JULIO: So . . .

GLADYS: I need to see what I'm doing.

JULIO: You're making tamales. You can make tamales in the dark.

GLADYS: That's what you think.

JULIO: That's what I know.

GLADYS: I'm getting older.

JULIO: I beg you . . .

GLADYS: What?

JULIO: Shut the windows and close the shutters. Please.

GLADYS: If I do, I'll have to turn on the lights.

JULIO: Who gives a rat's ass?

GLADYS: I do.

JULIO: In a socialist country, you don't have to pay for electricity.

GLADYS: But things wear out.

JULIO: You even want to have light bulbs from 1958.

GLADYS: No. Those burned out in 1961.

JULIO: Close the fucking shutters!

GLADYS: Look at this house.

JULIO: Close them for me.

GLADYS: The reason why this house looks the same, in this kind of condition, after twelve years . . . is because I am careful.

JULIO: It's because you are obsessed with the past.

GLADYS: No, I'm not.

JULIO: You're wearing her clothes.

GLADYS: I am sure she wears the latest fashion. Why waste a dress?

JULIO: The style now is above the knee.

GLADYS: I don't care.

JULIO: You should look good. Your husband is an important man.

GLADYS: He's sub-minister of transportation. What's the big deal?

JULIO: In a country where everybody takes a bus, and buys gasoline from him . . .

GLADYS: The government, not him.

JULIO: He's a big deal.

GLADYS: I still have to watch over this house. That's still my job.

JULIO: Do you get paid for it?

GLADYS: There's a blockade. She's not allowed to send me money.

JULIO: I thought she went to Paris.

GLADYS: No.

JULIO: From Europe, you can send money.

GLADYS: She's in Miami.

JULIO: Do you know this for sure?

GLADYS: That's what her aunt told me.

JULIO: Before she died?

GLADYS: Yes. She used to send me word via her aunt.

(Julio gives Gladys a funny look.)

She's always thinking about this house, about us.

JULIO: I don't give a fuck about her. She doesn't have to live here! Using everything they left behind till it stops working. Not being able to buy anything new 'cause they don't let anyone but the Russians trade with us . . . And you're supposed to want to do anything for that rich bitch?

GLADYS: Don't call her a bitch. You're in her house.

JULIO: It's your house now.

GLADYS: It will always be her house.

JULIO: You sleep in her bedroom.

GLADYS: Only in the summer, because it's cooler.

JULIO: Why do you waste your time?

GLADYS: What do you mean?

JULIO: Saving all of this for her.

GLADYS: I made a vow. I swore to her. I keep my promises.

JULIO: You're obsessed with her. She took her mink and she never looked back.

GLADYS: I won't ever believe that.

JULIO: She's never coming back.

GLADYS: She will. Someday, when the blockade ends.

JULIO: Sure.

GLADYS: It hurts me when you say stuff like that.

JULIO: Sorry.

GLADYS: Her family was very good to me.

JULIO: I know.

GLADYS: They took a little cleaning girl from Regla and gave her books.

JULIO: Yes, I know.

GLADYS: I had never read a novel till I met her mother.

JULIO: Of course.

GLADYS: They were good to all of us.

JULIO: They treated you like family. I know.

GLADYS: When I married Carlos . . .

JULIO: They hired him as a chauffeur. I know.

GLADYS: Just like that. To help us.

JULIO: And he took the job.

GLADYS: Yes. Of course.

JULIO: And now he's up there.

GLADYS: Because of the revolution. Without the revolution he'd still be a chauffeur. Pity.

JULIO: You're sorry he got ahead?

GLADYS: Ruined my life.

JULIO: Is that why you wait for her?

GLADYS: On the last day, she told me she was my friend. Can you believe that?

JULIO: It's an easy thing to say when you're exiting.

GLADYS: She meant it.

JULIO: Has she ever written you a letter?

GLADYS: She is the only person that has never betrayed me. Carlos betrayed me as you know.

JULIO: Yes. With his girlfriend . . .

GLADYS: Don't say her name.

JULIO: Fine.

GLADYS: Even in her silence. Adria does not betray me.

JULIO: That's how you see things.

GLADYS: Yes.

JULIO: When was the last time you had direct contact with her?

GLADYS: You know.

JULIO: New Year's Eve, 1958.

GLADYS: Actually, by the time she left, it was 1959. It was past midnight.

JULIO: And time stopped in this kitchen forever.

GLADYS: No.

JULIO: No?

GLADYS: I can feel time pass by.

JULIO: Then why don't you forget her?

GLADYS: She has not forgotten me.

JULIO: Rich people forget things.

GLADYS: What do you know about rich people?

JULIO: What I read about them from Marx.

GLADYS: Fidel is rich.

JULIO: I know.

GLADYS: He's no saint.

JULIO: He gave little poor girls from Regla the chance to read novels.

GLADYS: The ones he wanted them to read.

JULIO: Just like Adria and her mother.

(Julio looks timidly out the window.)

Please, Gladys, please, close the shutters.

GLADYS: Why?

JULIO: The secret police.

GLADYS: What?

JULIO: First close the shutters, please.

(Gladys closes the window shutters.)

Darkness, comfortable darkness.

GLADYS: There's comfort in sunlight also.

JULIO: For some people.

GLADYS: For decent people.

JULIO: Sometimes I hear El Morro Castle in the dark.

GLADYS: What?

JULIO: At night. Calling me. Telling me, "You will die inside my darkness."

GLADYS: El Morro Castle is a lighthouse.

JULIO: And a jail.

GLADYS: Like everything in this country, it serves two purposes.

JULIO: They take you down a long corridor, with long skinny windows, about three feet apart, looking out into the darkness of the bay. Not the lights of the city.

GLADYS: I had a feeling you were coming today. That's why I started making tamales.

JULIO: Really?

GLADYS: I grated the corn myself, Julio.

JULIO: Carlos didn't help you?

GLADYS: He's too busy being a big shot.

JULIO: Of course.

GLADYS: Big man in the communist party.

JULIO: Yes, he is.

GLADYS: Who would've thought?

JULIO: Many people.

GLADYS: I couldn't tell.

JULIO: You were too busy cooking.

GLADYS: I didn't know how big the change would be.

JULIO: At least you got to keep the house.

GLADYS: Yes.

JULIO: Yes.

GLADYS: Help me make these. Cooking relaxes a . . .

JULIO: Gladys, take a peek through the shutters and see if anyone is looking in.

GLADYS: What?

JULIO: Please.

GLADYS: No.

JULIO: No? Why?

GLADYS: I have to finish making the tamales.

JULIO: Fine.

(Julio looks.)

Fuck! He's still there. This time they mean business. Fuck!

GLADYS: Tamales are all we have left from the indigenous people that once lived here. Their souls comfort us when we eat tamales. And you need comfort, Cousin.

JULIO: Yes, I do.

GLADYS: These tamales will bring you peace.

JULIO: I hope you're right.

GLADYS: I know I'm right.

JULIO: Yes?

GLADYS: Yes.

JULIO: Pray for me, Cousin.

GLADYS: I'll feed you. That's better than praying.

JULIO: I hope so.

GLADYS: Turn on the lights. I can't see what I'm cooking.

JULIO: Yes.

(Julio turns on the lights.)

GLADYS: You shouldn't wear such loud clothes.

JULIO: I like them.

GLADYS: Those pants, Julio. No wonder people follow you around.

JULIO: They're in style.

GLADYS: Where? Not here.

JULIO: In the rest of the world.

GLADYS: Not in Russia.

JULIO: No.

GLADYS: Not in China.

JULIO: No.

GLADYS: But in Paris, right?

JULIO: And in the United States.

GLADYS: But not here. And, Julio, you live here.

JULIO: No, not here. Only in a certain crowd.

GLADYS: It's better not to be noticed. Wear them in the privacy of your own house.

JULIO: I always liked style.

GLADYS: I know.

JULIO: You used to give me Adria's old *Vogue*s.

GLADYS: Yes, well.

JULIO: You know.

GLADYS: What?

JULIO: I know you know. About me . . .

GLADYS: Help me stuff the cornhusks, will you?

JULIO: Do you want me to tell you?

GLADYS: You're good at tying the cornhusks together.

JULIO: Do you want me to tell you why I'm being followed?

GLADYS: I went to El Morro Castle once, as a young girl. If you look out from it . . . to the horizon, you can tell the world is round.

JULIO: Do you?

(Pause.)

GLADYS: Do you need to tell me?

JULIO: What for?

GLADYS: Good.

JULIO: I think there's a part of you that knows already. You know about me.

GLADYS: I know you're my cousin and I love you.

JULIO: What else?

GLADYS: What?

JULIO: What else have you heard?

GLADYS: Nothing.

JULIO: Liar.

GLADYS: I don't like to listen to malicious rumors about my family.

JULIO: Maybe sometimes you should.

GLADYS: Stop being lazy and help me.

JULIO: Listen to me. Some things are rumors. Some things are facts.

GLADYS: So what?

JULIO: Fact: I never got married.

GLADYS: Fact: you never found the right girl.

JULIO: Fact: I don't know how to love a woman.

GLADYS: Fact: your first girlfriend broke your heart.

JULIO: Fact: the secret police are after me because of my improper conduct.

GLADYS: Because your pants are too tight?

JULIO: Much more.

GLADYS: Improper conduct is when a person behaves outside the norm.

JULIO: When did this country become so moralistic?

GLADYS: When Raul Castro went to China . . . and he asked how they handled their homosexual problem. They replied, "We kill them, throw them in the river and then let their bodies float down to town. So they can see what the punishment is for improper conduct." But Cuba, being more humanistic, just puts deviants in camps.

JULIO: So you're aware of what goes on in the world.

GLADYS: Yes, I am.

JULIO: Good.

GLADYS: Why?

JULIO: So you can understand.

GLADYS: What?

JULIO: Me.

GLADYS: You?

JULIO: I'm a deviant.

GLADYS: Marry someone.

JULIO: I can't.

GLADYS: Why not?

JULIO: Because I have fallen in love.

GLADYS: I see.

JULIO: And his family . . .

GLADYS: You've fallen in love with a man?

JULIO: He's almost a man.

GLADYS: Almost is not the same thing.

JULIO: For me it is.

GLADYS: Is he white?

JULIO: Yes.

GLADYS: Marry someone.

JULIO: No.

GLADYS: Save yourself.

(Carlos walks in. He has a beard now, which is graying. He wears a suit.)

CARLOS: Julio.

JULIO: Yes, Carlos.

CARLOS: Have you joined the Navy?

JULIO: Why do you say that, Carlos?

CARLOS: No man would wear pants like that for any other reason.

JULIO: I haven't joined the Navy.

CARLOS: Or have you just been visiting the docks?

GLADYS: Carlos, leave Julio alone.

CARLOS: Really?

GLADYS: Really.

CARLOS: I can say whatever I want, in my house.

GLADYS: If you had one.

CARLOS: Had what?

GLADYS: A house.

CARLOS: I do.

GLADYS: Really?

CARLOS: Yes.

GLADYS: Where?

CARLOS: Here. This is my house.

GLADYS: Really. You're full of fairy tales today!

CARLOS: The government gave it to me as a gift.

GLADYS: Was it theirs to give?

CARLOS: What do you mean?

GLADYS: The owner of the house put me in charge of it.

CARLOS: This house belongs to the people.

GLADYS: Aren't I the people?

CARLOS: You're no longer the boss.

GLADYS: I was never the boss.

CARLOS: Really?

GLADYS: Really! Absolutely. No doubt in my mind!

CARLOS: Funny, that's not how I remember it.

JULIO: Your memory is selective, Carlos.

CARLOS: What do you mean by that?

JULIO: You forget that you were without a job before you married
     my cousin. And then suddenly, like magic, you had a uniform
     and became a chauffeur.

CARLOS: Don't start fucking around with me, Julio. If you know
     what's good for you.

JULIO: All right.

CARLOS: Good.

GLADYS: Big man in town now.

CARLOS: Yes, I am. You should be proud.

GLADYS: I would be if you hadn't betrayed me.

CARLOS: Betrayal is in the eye of the beholder. Truth is sometimes called betrayal.

GLADYS: And adultery?

CARLOS: A way of life.

GLADYS: Ah.

(Gladys makes the tamales.)

You cheat on me with someone younger and I'm supposed to think that's revolutionary also.

CARLOS: I got the memory of an elephant. I know how much shit I had to swallow before the revolution.

JULIO: How do you remember it, Carlos?

GLADYS: Incorrectly, that's how he remembers it.

CARLOS: I don't think so.

GLADYS: I know so.

CARLOS: I remember that you were a totalitarian in this kitchen . . .

GLADYS: And with good reason.

CARLOS: And all you care about, and all you know about is this house, this corner of El Vedado. Do you have any idea what's going on outside?

GLADYS: Charity from the Russians.

JULIO: See? More than you thought, Carlos.

CARLOS: Charity from the Russians. Is that all you see?

GLADYS: Yes.

CARLOS: No. You stupid bitch! The people's revolution, that's what's going on outside this house. That's what's going on in this country. There's a dialectical explosion going on. It has rocked the world. We've said no to capitalism. No to the class system. That's what's going on. And there's no room for a dictator, not even in a kitchen. And that's why you hate me . . . 'Cause now I'm your equal.

GLADYS: Equal? No.

CARLOS: Yes. Not the guy you got a job for. I'm part of the greatest revolution on the face of this earth.

JULIO: Really, Carlos?

GLADYS: There are a million Cubans in Miami that disagree with
you.

CARLOS: Who the hell do you know in Miami?

GLADYS: People.

CARLOS: Name them.

GLADYS: Never mind . . .

JULIO: I'll answer for you.

CARLOS: You're talking for her now?

JULIO: Well, for example . . .

CARLOS: Yes?

GLADYS: The people who own this house.

JULIO: That's right.

GLADYS: Adria Santana and her husband, Pablo. And whatever child
they had.

CARLOS: Will you ever evolve beyond this kitchen?

GLADYS: I have evolved . . .

CARLOS: Really?

GLADYS: Yes. I no longer sleep with you.

JULIO: That's right.

CARLOS: Personal, sexual politics, still bourgeois.

JULIO: Really?

GLADYS: The emancipation of the female is not a bourgeois concept.
It's revolutionary. Anarchistic, even.

JULIO: Good for you, Cousin.

CARLOS: You guard this house like a sphinx at the pyramids.

GLADYS: I keep my promises, my vows.

CARLOS: Then be a wife.

GLADYS: I wash your clothes, I feed you. I even care about you. I just
don't love you anymore.

JULIO: You broke her heart.

CARLOS: No.

JULIO: You cheated on her.

CARLOS: But I did not break her heart.

JULIO: What?

CARLOS: My cheating was a reaction to her broken heart.

GLADYS: Liar.

CARLOS: No.

JULIO: You are.

CARLOS: No. Adria. Adria Santana broke her heart. She never came back.

JULIO: Oh.

GLADYS: She will.

(Julio sneaks a look out the window.)

JULIO: He's still out there.

CARLOS: Who?

GLADYS: Don't tell him anything.

CARLOS: Tell me.

JULIO: Well . . .

GLADYS: Don't.

JULIO: Maybe he can help me.

GLADYS: No.

CARLOS: Come on.

JULIO: Someone from the secret police has been following me.

CARLOS: 'Cause you are a faggot!

GLADYS: No.

JULIO: Yes, Carlos. Because I'm a faggot.

CARLOS: I know. With pants like those, what else could you be?

JULIO: I have the right to wear whatever I want.

CARLOS: You do not.

JULIO: Yes, I do.

GLADYS: Julio, Carlos is right. For once he's right. Why show your weakness?

JULIO: Because it's not a weakness.

CARLOS: See the problem we're faced with?

JULIO: What?

CARLOS: A society that can't be weak. Do you see that Gladys?

JULIO: Don't answer.

GLADYS: Go upstairs. To the master bedroom.

CARLOS: The one you keep me out of.

GLADYS: Because you have a mistress.

CARLOS: A man like me has a right to a mistress.

JULIO: I'm the one in trouble.

GLADYS: Yes. And I'm going to get you out of it.

CARLOS: Are you?

GLADYS: Listen to me, Julio. In her husband's closet. You know which one that is?

CARLOS: The one on the right hand side of the room.

GLADYS: The one to the left of the bathroom. In it, there are many proper pants and shirts and shoes. Take one of each. Put them on. I'm going to let you borrow them. So they won't know it's you, when you leave this house.

CARLOS: Also a hat.

GLADYS: Yes, a Panama.

CARLOS: Stick all that fucking hair into it.

JULIO: He was bigger than me.

CARLOS: Wear a belt.

GLADYS: Belts are in the chest of drawers by the window.

JULIO: I'll look fat in his clothes.

GLADYS: You will look like a man.

CARLOS: Do it quickly, Julio. You're the only person she has ever given anything to, from this holy place.

JULIO: Gladys?

GLADYS: Do it!

JULIO: I'll be back.

(Julio exits.)

GLADYS: Will you help him?

CARLOS: He parades himself in every part of town.

GLADYS: I need you to help him.

CARLOS: He's having an affair with an eighteen-year-old white boy, whose father works at the Ministry of Information.

GLADYS: Is his father trusted by the party?

CARLOS: His character is questionable.

GLADYS: Then save my cousin.

CARLOS: Fine. Done.

GLADYS: Thank you.

CARLOS: We're still family.

GLADYS: Yes.

CARLOS: He's gonna have to start behaving differently.

GLADYS: I'll speak to his mother.

CARLOS: Tamales! Will you let me eat as many as I want?

GLADYS: Yes.

CARLOS: Well.

GLADYS: All of them, if you want.

CARLOS: You're really grateful?

GLADYS: Yes, I am.

CARLOS: Finally.

GLADYS: You have me where you want me.

CARLOS: I still love you.

GLADYS: You should.

(Gladys starts to cook the tamales. Throwing the wrapped ones into a pot of boiling water.)

CARLOS: There is one thing.

GLADYS: Yes.

CARLOS: My girlfriend . . .

GLADYS: Yes.

CARLOS: I have one, as you know.

GLADYS: Yes.

CARLOS: And I need—

GLADYS: What? You want two mistresses now?

CARLOS: No.

GLADYS: Then?

CARLOS: Well . . .

GLADYS: Yes?

CARLOS: My girlfriend is pregnant.

GLADYS: Bastard!

CARLOS: Come on.

GLADYS: You cheating bastard!

CARLOS: Yes, I am.

GLADYS: I hate you. I hate you. I hate you. God, I hate you!

CARLOS: So I guess it was you who wasn't fertile.

GLADYS: Maybe she cheated on you.

CARLOS: Never.

GLADYS: Sure of yourself.

CARLOS: That girl worships me.

GLADYS: Or your position.

CARLOS: My position is me.

GLADYS: True. Why can't I stop hating you?

CARLOS: Unrequited passion.

GLADYS: Passion? Do not flatter yourself.

CARLOS: All right.

GLADYS: Please. Passion? Please.

CARLOS: I want her to move in here. I want my child to live in the best I can give.

GLADYS: You're nuts.

CARLOS: I think we could all live in my house together.

GLADYS: This is not your house.

CARLOS: I tried to find her another place. But finding housing is impossible in La Habana.

GLADYS: Even for an important man like you?

CARLOS: Yes.

GLADYS: Or are you just a third-tier Fidelista?

CARLOS: Powerful enough to have somebody put away.

GLADYS: Like my cousin.

CARLOS: Put in a camp.

GLADYS: You would do that?

CARLOS: Yes, I would.

GLADYS: If I don't give you what you want.

CARLOS: That's right.

GLADYS: You think you can threaten me.

CARLOS: I'm asking you to be logical.

GLADYS: This house is not ours. I take care of it. I don't want your brat and your girlfriend bringing their filth into this place.

CARLOS: You know you're being stupid. The only reason we live alone in this house. The only reason any other family has not moved in. Is because of me. My power, my influence. Favors I've asked for. That's why you live in this house. Because of me . . . admit it.

GLADYS: I have my pride.

CARLOS: If you don't do this . . .

GLADYS: You won't lift a finger to help him?

CARLOS: I will point the finger to destroy him.

GLADYS: What are you?

CARLOS: A man who can do in his castle whatever he wants.

GLADYS: Really?

CARLOS: Yes. I'm the boss here.

GLADYS: Not while I'm alive.

CARLOS: Is that your answer?

GLADYS: Point the finger, Carlos.

CARLOS: Bitch.

GLADYS: And live with the guilt.

CARLOS: Stupid, stupid girl.

GLADYS: Proud woman.

CARLOS: You'll never learn.

(Carlos leaves.)

GLADYS: Cook, Gladys. Cook.

(She takes out the cooked tamales and she puts more tamales into a pot.)

You must cook.

(Carlos walks back in.)

CARLOS: I just told your cousin how you betrayed him.

GLADYS: I'm not betraying myself for any man.

CARLOS: You're black. Do you know that?

GLADYS: Yes. I do.

CARLOS: You're not her.

GLADYS: Yes, I know.

(Gladys serves Carlos a plate of tamales. Carlos eats.)

But in her house, in her clothes, I feel like I am.

(Julio walks in.)

JULIO: How could you?

GLADYS: Run out into the streets, Julio. Try to get on a raft. When you get to Miami, Adria will help you.

JULIO: Carlos could've saved me.

GLADYS: Save yourself.

JULIO: But . . .

GLADYS: No more buts.

JULIO: I need . . .

GLADYS: No more words.

JULIO: You can't . . .

GLADYS: No words. Run.

JULIO: I . . .

GLADYS: Save yourself.

JULIO: I don't know how.

GLADYS: Go.

JULIO: I'm scared.

GLADYS: Stop it.

JULIO: I'm scared.

GLADYS: Be a man.

JULIO: They won't let me.

GLADYS: Get out!

JULIO: I want to eat dinner first.

(Julio takes a tamale, puts it on a plate and eats.)

GLADYS: They'll be coming after you soon.

JULIO: Tell Carlos that you're sorry.

GLADYS: But I'm not.

JULIO: You won't save me.

GLADYS: No.

JULIO: You never loved me.

GLADYS: Sometimes there are things bigger than love.

JULIO: I hate you.

GLADYS: Fine.

JULIO: You could've helped me.

GLADYS: Go.

JULIO: But . . .

GLADYS: No more meals here.

(Gladys takes the plate away from Julio.)

JULIO: God!
GLADYS: You should've married somebody.
JULIO: I thought the revolution was also going to include me.
GLADYS: You were wrong.
JULIO: God!
GLADYS: Get out of my kitchen.
JULIO: Yes.
GLADYS: Go to Miami.
JULIO: Sure.
GLADYS: Adria will help you.
JULIO: You could've saved me.
GLADYS: The tamales are going to get over-cooked.

(Julio leaves. Gladys takes the tamales out of the pot. Carlos is still eating. She opens one of the tamales and tries to eat it.)

Too much salt.

(She takes another taste. Carlos goes to the phone, dials.)

CARLOS: He's yours.

(Carlos hangs up the phone. Goes back to the table and eats.)

GLADYS: No. Bitter. The corn must have been bitter. Not my fault. Not my fault.

(Blackout.)

ACT THREE

The kitchen, 1997. The kitchen still looks the same. But it has now faded with time. It is lunchtime. Gladys has turned the house into a "paladar"—the Cuban word for a restaurant inside a private home. Gladys is now in her seventies, but still looks good and younger than she is. She is dressed extremely well. Carlos is wearing a white apron and is chopping onions. His daughter, Rosa, a dark skinned girl in her twenties, is chopping garlic.

CARLOS: It's getting to be more and more work.

GLADYS: What is?

CARLOS: You know.

GLADYS: The paladar?

CARLOS: This cooking business.

GLADYS: Thank God.

ROSA: They all want Gladys' garlic chicken.

GLADYS: That's good, dear.

CARLOS: Why?

GLADYS: It's an easy dish to make. Just lots of oranges, limes, garlic, onions and some oregano. And then put it in the oven.

ROSA: You're right.

GLADYS: An easy way to make dollars.

CARLOS: It's not so we can make dollars, it's so we can survive.

ROSA: I want to do more than survive.

CARLOS: Careful, daughter. You're talking like a capitalist.

GLADYS: So? Where would we be without the tourists' dollars?

CARLOS: Living on my pension.

GLADYS: You mean starving on your pension?

CARLOS: We're a socialist society. We take care of each other.

GLADYS: With tourists and dollars.

CARLOS: It's all the blockade's fault.

GLADYS: It's all Fidel Castro's fault.

CARLOS: No it's not. Do not say one word against Fidel. I love the man.

GLADYS: After all these years you blame him for nothing?

CARLOS: He is my Adria.

GLADYS: Do not compare Adria to Fidel. Fidel has almost destroyed this country, and you know it.

CARLOS: He has not. The blockade made him dependent on the Russians. When the Russians abandoned us, we came to this special period . . .

GLADYS: Of starvation?

CARLOS: What?

GLADYS: You heard me.

CARLOS: We're not starving.

GLADYS: Like I said before, because of my cooking and the beauty of this house.

ROSA: You have to admit she's right.

CARLOS: She doesn't have to be arrogant.

GLADYS: Proud.

(*Carlos looks inside a small notebook.*)

CARLOS: How many reservations so far today?

ROSA: Ten for lunch.

CARLOS: Good. We're meeting our goals.

ROSA: Yes, we are!

CARLOS: I knew we would.

GLADYS: Now who's become a capitalist?

CARLOS: In this special period, we all have to change our way of surviving, but not our ideals.

GLADYS: What did your ideals get you?

CARLOS: Dignity.

GLADYS: And a city that is falling apart.

CARLOS: Fidel feels terrible about it.

GLADYS: He told you this?

CARLOS: The last time I talked with Fidel was thirty years ago.

GLADYS: At a gathering you took her mother to.

CARLOS: You were anti-communist.

GLADYS: Was that the reason?

CARLOS: You know it was.

GLADYS: Fine.

CARLOS: If Fidel says bring the tourists back . . .

ROSA: Then why not feed them, right Papi?

CARLOS: Right.

GLADYS: You, Carlos, should thank God and the Virgin Mother of Regla that I can still cook at my age.

CARLOS: So, ten reservations?

ROSA: Yes, as of this moment.

CARLOS: And there will be people that will just walk in.

ROSA: That's what always happens.

CARLOS: Yes.

GLADYS: And it's film festival time, don't forget that.

ROSA: I should have my camera ready.

GLADYS: Yes, you should.

CARLOS: I love having my picture taken with movie stars.

ROSA: We know you do.

GLADYS: Rosa, buy more film next time you're at the Nacional.

ROSA: I will, Gladys.

(The bell rings.)

CARLOS: Somebody's here early.

GLADYS: No one's rung that bell in more than thirty years.

CARLOS: What are you saying?

GLADYS: That no one's rung the bell in more than . . .

CARLOS: Must be Spaniards. They're always hungry.

(The bell rings.)

GLADYS: Aggressive.

CARLOS: Then they're German.

ROSA: I'll get it.

GLADYS: Remember, today we have chicken, lobster, pork, plantains and rum-flavored ice cream.

ROSA: Rum.

CARLOS: Yum!

ROSA: Keep your hands away from it, Papi.

CARLOS: I will.

ROSA: Promise?

CARLOS: I promise.

ROSA: Gladys, the day you decided to turn this place into a paladar . . .

GLADYS: I wish we could call it a restaurant.

ROSA: That's the day I knew you had genius in you.

GLADYS: Thank you, sweet girl. Why can't we call it a restaurant?

CARLOS: Restaurants are run by the government, not individuals.

GLADYS: Part of the insanity.

CARLOS: The logic of revolution.

GLADYS: It's a good thing I figured out a way around your revolutionary logic.

ROSA: We were one of the first paladars in the city. Now they are everywhere.

GLADYS: But my cooking is better.

CARLOS: It is. Better than any of the others.

ROSA: All the guide books agree.

GLADYS: Good.

CARLOS: Always thought she should've been a chef.

GLADYS: Did you? Did you really? Carlos!

CARLOS: You know I did.

GLADYS: You never helped me get out of this house.

CARLOS: Don't start.

(The bell rings.)

GLADYS: How did they know there was a bell? It's hidden.
ROSA: I better take care of the customers.
GLADYS: You do that, sweetie.

(Rosa leaves.)

CARLOS: I knew we'd be one happy family. But I had to wait till her mother died.
GLADYS: Her mother did not die. She went to Miami.
CARLOS: Dead to me.
GLADYS: You should forgive the ones that left.
CARLOS: Never!
GLADYS: Why not?
CARLOS: The blockade.
GLADYS: Forget the blockade.
CARLOS: It's the people in Miami's fault.
GLADYS: They really made something of themselves, didn't they?
CARLOS: The ruling class always survives.
GLADYS: Are you going to be a communist till the day you die?
CARLOS: Yes, I am.
GLADYS: Even though they never gave you what they promised you.
CARLOS: They tried.
GLADYS: How?
CARLOS: I know they tried. But the blockade . . .
GLADYS: You'll never learn. Stubborn.
CARLOS: That's why I still love you. You are just as stubborn.
GLADYS: Sure. I'm stubborn.
CARLOS: I will always love you for taking my Rosa in.
GLADYS: She's a sweet girl.
CARLOS: You raised her.
GLADYS: Yes, I did.
CARLOS: That's why she's a great worker.
GLADYS: Yes, she is.

CARLOS: Yes, she is.

GLADYS: Adria would've liked her.

CARLOS: I wouldn't have let my daughter work for Adria.

GLADYS: Only your wife?

CARLOS: I didn't like you working for her either. But we had no other choice back then.

GLADYS: We have no other choice now.

CARLOS: What are you talking about?

GLADYS: They're all coming back. And we wait on them. Tourists. What's changed?

CARLOS: My daughter is studying to be an engineer and this is our place.

GLADYS: For now.

CARLOS: That's a big difference. And Cuba belongs to us.

GLADYS: The proletariats?

CARLOS: Yes. People like us.

GLADYS: I don't know, everyone in power looks white to me.

CARLOS: Someday that will change.

GLADYS: And most of them are men. Old men like you.

CARLOS: Did you like anything about the revolution?

GLADYS: Yes. I liked that we remained Cuban. During Batista, we were becoming something else.

CARLOS: Now we are who we are.

GLADYS: That's right.

CARLOS: I love Fidel. I love the man.

GLADYS: With your lousy pension.

CARLOS: I would have understood hunger . . .

GLADYS: You never liked being hungry, Carlos.

CARLOS: But I didn't think he'd ever willingly let them back in.

GLADYS: The ones that left?

CARLOS: Yes. The traitors. The worms.

GLADYS: He needs their dollars. We need their dollars.

CARLOS: Not fair.

GLADYS: We always have needed their dollars.

CARLOS: Fuck them.

GLADYS: Can't live without rich people, if you want to eat well, Carlos.

CARLOS: I think now there's a chance that Adria will come back.

(Pause.)

GLADYS: Really?

CARLOS: Isn't that what you've been hoping for.

GLADYS: It would be the answer to my prayers.

CARLOS: Are you crazy?

GLADYS: She'd see that I kept my word; that I was faithful.

CARLOS: Faithful?

GLADYS: And she would thank me.

CARLOS: You think she is going to thank you?

GLADYS: She will! You'll see!

CARLOS: Jesus fucking Christ!

GLADYS: Why are you cursing Christ when you denied his existence for forty years?

CARLOS: What?

GLADYS: Why don't you say Karl fucking Marx?

(Gladys laughs.)

CARLOS: This is not a joke.

GLADYS: It all seems funny to me.

CARLOS: They'd want the house back. What would happen to your business? What would happen to our lives? We'd starve.

GLADYS: No, she'd give me a better pension than the one that Fidel gave you.

CARLOS: You're a fool.

GLADYS: No, I'm not. I know what people I can trust.

CARLOS: I don't want them coming here and taking away everything I earned.

GLADYS: Serves you right.

CARLOS: You really hate me, don't you?

GLADYS: Let them take what belongs to them. If they come back, I'll give it to them.

(Pause.)

CARLOS: Well . . . I think they will. The other day I was at our comrade Rolando's house . . .

GLADYS: The retired General down the street?

CARLOS: Yes, a man who gave his life for the revolution.

GLADYS: And he got a big fancy mansion as his reward.

CARLOS: That's right. This black Mercedes-Benz drove up, and this very . . . well . . . this dressed up sissy walked out of it, and it was the grandson of the guy that used to own the house. Rolando refused to let him in. He told Rolando to go fuck himself and walked into the house. Rolando says they will get it all back eventually.

GLADYS: Good.

(Rosa walks in.)

So, what's the order?

CARLOS: Come on. I'm ready.

ROSA: She's not sure she wants lunch.

GLADYS: Then why is she here? One comes here to eat.

ROSA: She just wants to take pictures.

GLADYS: We're not a museum.

CARLOS: Is she German?

ROSA: No.

GLADYS: French?

ROSA: No.

GLADYS: Canadian?

CARLOS: Italian?

ROSA: From The U.S. But she sounds like a Latina and her husband is a . . .

GLADYS: A couple?

ROSA: Yes.

GLADYS: Tell them they can't take pictures. Without ordering food.

ROSA: What?

GLADYS: They can take pictures, if they buy lunch. If they don't, then, no pictures.

ROSA: They seem nice.

GLADYS: No dollars, no pictures.

ROSA: What's the harm?

GLADYS: This is not a tourist site.

ROSA: But . . .

CARLOS: Gladys is right.

ROSA: Fine.

CARLOS: I'll go tell them.

ROSA: No, I will.

(The bell rings.)

CARLOS: Uppity.

ROSA: Yes.

GLADYS: She must be Cuban-American.

ROSA: Must be.

GLADYS: Is she wearing a lot of jewelry?

ROSA: No.

GLADYS: No? Now, that's odd.

CARLOS: Yes. They usually look like a walking jewelry store.

GLADYS: I hear they rent them, so they can show up looking rich.

CARLOS: That's also what I hear.

(The bell rings.)

ROSA: I better go.

(Rosa leaves.)

GLADYS: I think you're not chopping the onions fine enough.

CARLOS: Yes, I am.

GLADYS: A little finer, please.

CARLOS: So we've come full circle, haven't we?

GLADYS: What do you mean?

CARLOS: You get to boss me around in the kitchen again.

GLADYS: Yes.

CARLOS: You like it?

GLADYS: Yes, I do.

CARLOS: I thought so.

(Rosa walks in.)

GLADYS: So?

ROSA: She wants to take pictures of the bedrooms, the bathrooms and the kitchen.

GLADYS: Who the hell does she think she is?

ROSA: She said she owns this place.

GLADYS: She's come back.

CARLOS: Oh, my God!

GLADYS: How do I look? Bring her in here.

(Rosa leaves.)

Oh my God! Adria! Adria!

CARLOS: Ssshhhh.

GLADYS: Adria Santana . . .

CARLOS: It's happened.

GLADYS: Thank you, sweet Mary.

CARLOS: The world has gone around and come back in the same direction.

(Lourdes, Adria's daughter, walks in. She looks exactly like Adria. She has a camera. She is taking pictures.)

LOURDES: My God! It's as if I remembered it all, even the hallway in front of the kitchen.

ROSA: We have worked hard to keep it in shape.

(Lourdes walks back down the hallway and disappears.)

Wait a minute, the kitchen is this way.

LOURDES *(Offstage)*: The kitchen. One more picture of that window before I see the kitchen.

(Rosa goes to get Lourdes.)

GLADYS: Sometimes miracles do happen.

CARLOS: My God!

GLADYS: What?

CARLOS: Did you take a look at her. She hasn't aged. Look at us. We
have.

GLADYS: Plastic surgery, she was already talking about it before she
left La Habana.

CARLOS: The doctor is a miracle worker.

(Lourdes and Rosa walk back in.)

LOURDES: My mother, she kept it all alive in her mind. And I guess
I remember more of her stories than I thought. That's interesting.
I was listening after all.

ROSA: The kitchen is right in here.

GLADYS: Come into the kitchen. Please.

(Lourdes walks up to Gladys.)

I kept it the same for your return. Forty years. And I kept it
clean and in order for you, Adria.

LOURDES: Adria? I'm not—Who are you?

GLADYS: I've gotten old. I know. I'm sorry. I'm the cook.

LOURDES: The cook?

GLADYS: Oh my God! She doesn't recognize me. How can you not
recognize me? Señora!

CARLOS: I drove you everywhere.

LOURDES: You drove Adria?

GLADYS: Yes!

LOURDES: The cook and the chauffeur. Is that who you are?

GLADYS: Look at us. We waited for you.

LOURDES: You are the people who my mother told me about.

GLADYS: Your mother?

LOURDES: Yes. She told me.

ROSA: She's the daughter. Gladys. Adria's daughter.

GLADYS: The daughter? She had a daughter! I'm so happy. You look
just like her. As beautiful as Adria. What's your name dear?

LOURDES: Lourdes.

GLADYS: After your great aunt.

LOURDES: Yes, that's right. I never met her. She died here.

GLADYS: I have her picture, look. I saved this for you.

LOURDES: My great aunt?

GLADYS: Yes. She did . . . She did die here. Around 1966 . . . In August. August 31, 1966. That's right. Sometimes I think she died of loneliness. After everyone left, I tried to visit her every once in a while. But she stopped opening the door.

LOURDES: Loneliness?

GLADYS: I tried to explain to her that I was not a communist, but well . . . I'm afraid her mind had gone a little. Just like her mother's . . . your great-grandmother Soraya . . . like mother like daughter . . .

LOURDES: You know my heritage?

GLADYS: Like the back of my hand. Oh my God. Look at you, sweet little Lourdes. So brave to come all the way here and visit us. Isn't she brave, Carlos?

CARLOS: Maybe.

GLADYS: Sit down, Lourdes. Carlos, go get her husband.

CARLOS: It's moments like this that I wish I had faith.

GLADYS: You have Fidel. Go!

(Carlos starts to exit.)

LOURDES: Listen, thank you for showing me the house. Very nice of you. But I think I better go.

ROSA: Really, so soon?

LOURDES: I'm not really ready for this. I'm getting a little angry and I don't know why.

ROSA: There is nothing to be angry about.

LOURDES: Don't be naive.

ROSA: I'm not naive. There is nothing to be angry about.

LOURDES: What do you mean? There are decades of dictatorship to be angry about.

ROSA: Revolution.

LOURDES: What?

ROSA: Decades of revolution.

LOURDES: Right. Sorry.

GLADYS: Maybe we should go into the living room? You want some water, mango juice?

CARLOS: Rum?

LOURDES: I don't think so. You are being so friendly.

ROSA: We are very friendly.

CARLOS: We don't have a blockade against you.

ROSA: Papi!

(Carlos exits.
Gladys presents a photo album to Lourdes.)

GLADYS: I saved this for you. Your entire family is in here. And here is your grandmother.

LOURDES: Yes.

GLADYS: What a smart woman she was.

LOURDES: Really?

GLADYS: Well read.

LOURDES: I didn't know that about her.

GLADYS: No?

LOURDES: She was just someone with an accent.

GLADYS: And your grandfather.

LOURDES: He had hair.

GLADYS: Yes, he did.

ROSA: Handsome man.

GLADYS: All the men in her family were handsome. Lourdes.

LOURDES: Thank you for showing me the pictures. I don't think I need to see the rest of the house.

GLADYS: If you had been born here, you would have known me as well as you know your mother.

LOURDES: But I wasn't born here.

GLADYS: That's the tragedy.

LOURDES: I don't think so. Maybe for my mother but not for me. She felt so betrayed by everyone that stayed.

GLADYS: Not by me?

LOURDES: By everyone that stayed.

GLADYS: I did not betray her.

LOURDES: That's not what she believes.

GLADYS: What does she think? Tell me. Please!

LOURDES: That you were communists all along . . .

GLADYS: We were not!

LOURDES: You had been plotting all along.

GLADYS: What?

LOURDES: To take her house and keep it for yourselves.

GLADYS: I was not! Never. I never had a thought like that! Never! She was my best friend. I knew her when we were both girls. How could I ever? Ever even think of harming—

LOURDES: That you lied to her.

GLADYS: Lied to her? I worshipped your mother.

LOURDES: Really?

GLADYS: Really.

ROSA: She talks about her every day. She's been waiting for forty years for her return.

GLADYS: I have!

LOURDES: I don't know what to believe. It's a confusing country.

ROSA: No, it's a simple country.

GLADYS: No, it's not!

LOURDES: You agree with me?

GLADYS: Yes, must be hard to come back here, dear.

LOURDES: I was never here.

GLADYS: Right.

LOURDES: I'm an American.

ROSA: Are you?

LOURDES: Yes. I'm not my mother. I can forgive.

GLADYS: You can forgive me?

LOURDES: I want the album.

GLADYS: It's yours. Here. It's your family.

(Lourdes flips through the book.)

I've been waiting to give it back.

LOURDES: What?

GLADYS: The house.

ROSA: She has.

LOURDES: That's stretching it.

GLADYS: Why?

LOURDES: Look, it's easy to say you want to give it back. When there is no way to give it back. And you know it. There is no way that we could come back here to live . . .

ROSA: Because of the blockade.

LOURDES: Because of Fidel Castro. So the house is yours. Really. Fidel gave it to you. You lived in it. Not me. So please, just let me take a few pictures to take back to my mother. She'll cry over them. And hate you just a little bit more.

GLADYS: Hate me? Please tell her that I . . .

LOURDES: She won't want to know anything about you. Believe me. And really, how can you blame her?

GLADYS: I had nothing to do with the revolution.

LOURDES: To my mother, you are the revolution.

ROSA: She made sacrifices and cut corners to make sure the house got a fresh coat of paint once in a while. Their marriage was ruined over it . . . her cousin died in a camp because of it.

GLADYS: No, my cousin died in a camp because of us. Lourdes?

LOURDES: Yes?

GLADYS: Give me a moment. I deserve a moment.

LOURDES: Fine. *(Pause)* Yes?

GLADYS: I worked for your family since I was thirteen years old. My name is Gladys.

LOURDES: They never mentioned you by name.

GLADYS: So I am telling you my name. My name is Gladys.

LOURDES: Well . . . hello Gladys. Thank you for this glimpse into my mother. But I really should go.

GLADYS: How is your father?

LOURDES: He passed away.

GLADYS: How?

LOURDES: I don't think I have to answer that.

GLADYS: Please.

LOURDES: I'm trying. I really am trying. But I am getting so angry. It's irrational, isn't it? I don't like being irrational. But this whole Cuba thing is like a goddamned grenade. I didn't think that

I would be so angry. But . . . This should have been mine. My house. My life.

ROSA: But your mother decided to leave.

LOURDES: She had no choice.

ROSA: Perhaps.

GLADYS: No, Rosa. Adria was scared. The revolution was against people like her. But nobody knew that then. I didn't know that.

LOURDES: Maybe you did, maybe you didn't. But you sure have lived well, off my parents' misfortune.

GLADYS: I did not know Fidel was a communist. Believe me.

ROSA: She only stayed in this house to save it for your mother. Tell your mother that.

GLADYS: Please. Yes, tell her that. Good, Rosa. Thank you, Rosa.

ROSA: Anytime, Gladys. So you'll tell her?

LOURDES: I'll try.

ROSA: Good.

LOURDES: But . . . The conversation would only get as far as I went to the house and I met the cook, then she would walk away.

GLADYS: I loved Adria.

LOURDES: My mother is a very angry woman. Her only thought is revenge.

GLADYS: Against me?

LOURDES: Against anyone who stayed behind. She hasn't spoken to me for the past month, because I was coming here.

ROSA: Miami Mafia.

GLADYS: Be quiet, Rosa.

LOURDES: This can't have a happy ending. I should go.

ROSA: What made you come?

LOURDES: Well . . . unfinished business . . . It's strange to long for a past that was not yours.

GLADYS: Yes.

LOURDES: Sometimes I see Cuba in my dreams. Sometimes in my nightmares I am being taken away from here. Isn't that funny? I was never here until now.

ROSA: So you came to find out.

LOURDES: Yes.

GLADYS: Thank you.

LOURDES: I never thought I had the right to come here.

ROSA: Because of your mother?

LOURDES: Because of my entire family.

ROSA: I'm sorry.

LOURDES: But my husband . . . He is sort of a . . . well, a Democrat. He thought I should come and see my mother's world.

ROSA: You should.

GLADYS: Look at me then.

LOURDES: Why?

GLADYS: I was your mother's world.

LOURDES: And she never ever mentioned you by name. She's so bitter. Do you know what it was like to live with someone who became so bitter?

ROSA: How did your father die?

LOURDES: What?

ROSA: You owe her that much.

LOURDES: Do I really?

ROSA: Yes!

LOURDES: I'm not Cuban.

GLADYS: You were conceived here.

LOURDES: Really?

GLADYS: Yes.

LOURDES: Maybe that explains my dreams.

GLADYS: I remember the day your mother told me. New Year's Eve, 1958. I was in the kitchen. We were throwing a big party . . . I was making lime ice cream. She held my hand and told me. We were that close. She told me before she told your father. That's how much we meant to each other. That's the night she left. The night she asked me to keep this place the same for her. Till she returned. Haven't I done a good job? Lourdes?

LOURDES: My father died in Africa. They were there protecting some of Batista's oil interests. He died in her arms after his birthday party in 1972. She even blames that on Fidel.

ROSA: She should blame Batista. Why doesn't anyone blame Batista for anything?

LOURDES: That's true, he was a dictator.

ROSA: Do you believe us?

LOURDES: Yes, I think so.

GLADYS: I am so happy you decided to come back.

LOURDES: Good.

GLADYS: Yes, and I am going to make you flan with twelve eggs. Your mother loved my flan.

LOURDES: I bet she did.

GLADYS: It is like looking at her. Like I am finally within her eyesight again.

(Pause.)

Let me make you some café.

LOURDES: Yes.

GLADYS: Good.

(Gladys goes to make café.)

ROSA: Are you all right?

LOURDES: I don't know.

ROSA: You don't know?

LOURDES: I feel like I'm betraying her. If I understand you. I betray her. You see? I should go.

GLADYS: Where does she live now?

LOURDES: In East Hampton. She married again.

GLADYS: Good.

LOURDES: Good? I don't know. She lives a wasted life. I don't want to end up like that. Doing nothing with my life.

(Carlos walks back in.)

CARLOS: Your husband is waiting for you in the car.

GLADYS: He doesn't want to have lunch?

CARLOS: I don't think so.

LOURDES: He's like that.

GLADYS: We're a very famous paladar. We're in all the guidebooks.

ROSA: It would be on the house.

CARLOS: For sure.

LOURDES: Thank you, but . . .

ROSA: A free meal.

LOURDES: I can't.

GLADYS: Please.

LOURDES: My husband is very picky about food. He thinks in third world countries you should only eat at the hotels.

ROSA: Ah, well. Not that liberal. I should have guessed.

LOURDES: He tries.

GLADYS: My food is clean. My food is the talk of all La Habana.

LOURDES: My husband is from Boston.

GLADYS: Tell him he's insulting me!

LOURDES: He has his ways.

ROSA: And you?

LOURDES: I don't think I can be a guest at my mother's house. Eat at the table that was stolen from her. I can't go that far. I'm sorry.

ROSA: I see.

GLADYS: I did not steal anything!

LOURDES: Gladys, would you like me to take a picture of you to give my mother?

GLADYS: No.

LOURDES: Why not?

GLADYS: I'm not a tourist attraction.

LOURDES: This house is in the guide books.

GLADYS: But I am not.

LOURDES: Are you sure?

GLADYS: I am sure.

CARLOS: Tell me dear . . .

LOURDES: What?

CARLOS: Is your mother still rich?

LOURDES: I don't have to answer that.

CARLOS: Marx teaches us, that class is the real nationality, not religion, not country. It is what truly rules us, that the bourgeoisie, that's you, when they go to another place; they will always retain their status. So has she—your mother?

LOURDES: She is not as rich as she was here. All right?

CARLOS: But does she still have a maid?

LOURDES: Of course.

CARLOS: A cook?

LOURDES: Of course.

GLADYS: Enough.

CARLOS: We struggled . . . while they played. While they sold this country to gangsters, your family.

LOURDES: My family worked hard for their money. How can you insult them? You . . . who just . . . took and took.

ROSA: You are the one that is insulting us.

LOURDES: Because I won't eat here?

ROSA: No. Because you do not see the history you are facing.

LOURDES: It's not my history. I want nothing to do with my mother's history.

ROSA: Liar! You came here with your mind made up. And you cannot face the fact that we are not what you expected.

CARLOS: The ruling class always looks the other way. Remember that, daughter. They treat us well, when it's convenient for them. You won't accept what we are willing to give you.

LOURDES: And what's that?

ROSA: We are offering you love.

LOURDES: Love.

CARLOS: The love of Cuba. The love we feel for you.

LOURDES: I am not Cuban.

GLADYS: You will always be Cuban. This is where your life began.

LOURDES: You believe that?

GLADYS: Yes.

LOURDES: But, do you love me, or my money?

ROSA: How can you say that? Is that what happens in the United States, everything is about money?

LOURDES: Everything is about money here.

ROSA: No!

LOURDES: Yes. This new period? Is about how you cannot survive without the dollar.

ROSA: No. What's going on here has nothing to do with dollars. Don't you see?

LOURDES: I think it does. You used my mother's house, my mother's past. The most precious part of her memories, her youth, her home. You took it and you turned it into a restaurant. I'm surprised you didn't turn it into a whorehouse.

GLADYS: Get out of my house!

LOURDES: Your house?

GLADYS: Yes, my history, my house!

LOURDES: So that's what you really think. My mother was right.

GLADYS: Not until today.

LOURDES: What?

GLADYS: I didn't think this was my house, until I met you.

LOURDES: Because I don't want to eat your food?

GLADYS: Get out of here!

LOURDES: Why should I?

CARLOS: You all left.

LOURDES: Who left?

CARLOS: The ruling class.

LOURDES: My mother?

CARLOS: And your father.

LOURDES: His life was on the line.

CARLOS: Maybe.

LOURDES: He worked for Batista. He had to go.

CARLOS: He was a worm.

LOURDES: A worm?

CARLOS: A worm that was rotting Cuba.

LOURDES: Stop it!

GLADYS: No Carlos, tell her.

LOURDES: What?

GLADYS: She should know the truth.

LOURDES: You want to know the truth?

CARLOS: From your point of view?

LOURDES: Yes!

CARLOS: No!

GLADYS: I do.

LOURDES: Fine! My mother always said, "Imagine my house, my bathroom, my bed, being lived in, slept on, by a bunch of niggers."

CARLOS: You arrogant white bitch.

LOURDES: That's what my mother always said.

CARLOS: You want to know why your mother left? They were afraid you'd have to go to school with someone like my daughter. There was a saying in Cuba before the revolution. It went, "Go to white." Marry up. Marry someone lighter. So your children can end up white.

LOURDES: And what's the saying now? "Go to black"?

ROSA: No. The revolution changed all that. My color does not matter.

LOURDES: Yes it does. You have to look mulatta . . . so you can look exotic to some middle-aged German man. So you can sell yourself for twenty dollars.

GLADYS: She does not sell herself. My daughter does not and will never sell herself.

CARLOS: That's why we had a revolution.

LOURDES: Really? They should write a book about her. You must be the only one.

ROSA: I am not the only one.

CARLOS: My daughter is going to be an engineer!

LOURDES: And what will you build anything with?

ROSA: What?

LOURDES: What money? What materials?

ROSA: My pride, and my mind; which are far superior to yours.

LOURDES: Well . . . Really . . . Are they?

ROSA: Yes. What do you think about?

LOURDES: Many things.

ROSA: Name some.

LOURDES: That losing this house ruined my mother's chance for happiness. She has been homesick all her life.

GLADYS: She never wrote me a letter. Never once tried to reach me. She handed me seven hundred dollars and expected me to keep this place intact for forty years. And as the years went by, I kept believing in her loyalty. I never even allowed myself to dream of a way to escape any of this. Because I wanted her to have her house when she returned, to have a place she could recognize and feel safe in. And here it is. I did it.

LOURDES: She's never coming back.

GLADYS: I don't care anymore.

ROSA: If you're not buying lunch, you better go. This is a business. And we've got work to do.

LOURDES: You're kicking me out?

ROSA: Yes. Yes, I am. Get out!

LOURDES: It used to be beautiful. I can tell. Now it's ruined.

(Lourdes is about to take a photo of Gladys.)

ROSA: Don't you fucking dare.

(Lourdes walks away. Rosa follows her out.)

GLADYS: A cold reality has just left the room.

CARLOS: Finally, you understand the revolution.

(Rosa walks back in.)

GLADYS: She called me a nigger. Rosa? She thought I was a nigger. Not a friend . . . never even mentioned my name . . . once she left, she never said Gladys ever again.

ROSA: Let her go. Please, let the past go.

GLADYS: What a fool I've been.

CARLOS: No.

GLADYS: Why not?

CARLOS: You kept it all going.

GLADYS: Have I?

ROSA: All of it. For forty years. For us. We have the most popular paladar in all of La Habana.

GLADYS: Yes, we do.

ROSA: That's right.

CARLOS: I think we should have a better name for it than just our address.

ROSA: I always thought that.

CARLOS: Yes. I agree.

ROSA: We are going to call it "Gladys' Place."

CARLOS: Good.

GLADYS: Why not?

CARLOS: Yes.

ROSA: I'll get an artist to make a sign.

GLADYS: What time is it?

ROSA: Almost noon.

GLADYS: Come on. We've got to get those chickens in the oven.

ROSA: Yes, we do.

GLADYS: Come, Carlos. Time to work.

ROSA: We gotta get the chickens ready.

CARLOS: Yes, we do.

GLADYS: Carlos, keep chopping the onions.

CARLOS: I will.

(They start to prepare the food. Rosa takes out a notebook.)

ROSA: So, how many lemons?

GLADYS: What?

ROSA: For each chicken?

GLADYS: Around two.

(Rosa writes it down.)

Why are you writing it down?

ROSA: 'Cause I want to learn every recipe.

GLADYS: You do? Why?

ROSA: 'Cause I will try to be as good as you are.

CARLOS: Why?

ROSA: 'Cause I'm going to be a cook.

CARLOS: You're going to be an engineer.

ROSA: What good would that do me?

GLADYS: What?

CARLOS: My daughter is going to be a professional.

ROSA: A professional cook. Lourdes is right. What can we build anything with? The future for now is tourism. Even Fidel knows that. And I'd rather be a cook than a whore.

CARLOS: Don't talk like that in front of me.

GLADYS: Two lemons, half an orange, half a lime. Three spoonfuls of oregano and a little cumin, that's my trick, four cloves of

garlic and lard placed underneath the skin, salt and pepper . . .
strawberry.

ROSA: What?

GLADYS: It wasn't lime. It was strawberry in 1959.

CARLOS: This is just a special period.

GLADYS: Right.

CARLOS: This is not the end.

GLADYS: Do me a favor, Rosa . . .

ROSA: Anything . . .

GLADYS: When you learn everything from me . . . because I will
teach you every trick . . .

ROSA: Thank you.

GLADYS: Become a cook at a big fancy hotel.

(Rosa turns on the radio. They prepare the food.
Blackout.)

END OF PLAY

CROCODILE EYES

For Crystal Field

Production History

Crocodile Eyes made its world professional premiere at Theater for the New City (Crystal Field, Executive Director) in New York City and opened on April 22, 1999. It was directed by Eduardo Machado; set design was by Mark Marcante; lighting design was by Jon D. Andreadakis; and costume design was by David Obele (inspired by the works of Miguel Narros). The production stage manager was David Obele. It was performed by:

TOMAS	Victor Argo
FELIPE	Tom Soper
MAXIMILIAN	Ron Riley
JAIME	Jerry Jaffe
JOAQUIN	Joe Quintero
ADAM	Rolando Morales
PONCIA	Crystal Field
PEPE	Ed Vassallo
ADELA	Heather Hill
ANGUSTIAS	Tatyana Yassukovich

The final draft of *Crocodile Eyes* was subsequently performed by the Columbia University School of the Arts MFA Acting Class of 2005. It was directed by Eduardo Machado; set design was by Christopher Muller; lighting design was by Beverly Emmons; sound design was by Tony Gaballe; music composition was by Michael Moricz; and dramaturgy was by Megan Smith. The stage manager was Tom Talyor. It was performed by:

TOMAS	Justin Badger
FELIPE	Fri Forjindam
MAXIMILIAN	Jeff Clarke
JAIME	Daniel Irizarry
JOAQUIN	Marty Keiser
ADAM	Rebecca Lingafelter
PONCIA	Shelly Gershoni
PEPE	Robert Johanson
ADELA	Jessica Kaye
ANGUSTIAS	Elena Mulroney
MARIA JOSEFA	Stacy Parker
AMELIA	Greta Newgren

Playwright's Note

The set should be a raked stage painted enamel black. In the back, there are three dark green doors. No naturalistic set, please! No trees, no dirt, no Spanish tiles. There are only three black benches. No accents. (Except the ones the actors have naturally. Hopefully totally diverse. From English accents to Spanish to American.) The only props are the ones indicated. Angustias and Adela can have fans. The men can and should smoke. Thank you. Less is more.

ACT ONE

Outside Bernarda Alba's house, 1936. The patio. Upstage, three dark green doors lead to the house; the shutters are down. The sun is coming down hard today. Bells are ringing. The men (Maximilian, Felipe, Joaquin, Adam, Tomas and Jaime) sit on the patio drinking lemonade; they are of all ages. They are all dressed in black and gray; they have come from a funeral. They are tough men. They have spent their lives working in the fields, but today, even for them, the sun is coming down hard and hot.

TOMAS: Jesus. It's hot, goddamn . . .

FELIPE: Don't say the word, she'll hear you.

MAXIMILIAN: And we don't want her angry.

JAIME: I'm sure they are going to serve us lunch.

TOMAS: They must be getting lunch ready.

ADAM: Of course. Lamb, I bet.

MAXIMILIAN: No, pork.

FELIPE: Maybe sausages.

ADAM: Goat!

TOMAS: She's inside those cold walls. Cool and fanning herself not cooking.

MAXIMILIAN: Don't say that. I know she is cooking. I can smell it. Can you smell it, Felipe?

FELIPE: No.

TOMAS: Well, I can.

JOAQUIN: Where the hell is Pepe?

TOMAS: Which Pepe?

JOAQUIN: El Romano . . .

TOMAS: That son of a . . .

FELIPE: Don't say that word either . . . Unless you want to have a fist fight in the middle of a wake.

TOMAS: Why?

FELIPE: If Pepe is not here. Why call his mother a . . .

TOMAS: Bitch?

ADAM: Hey.

TOMAS: We don't want a fight.

FELIPE: I bet we are going to have bread pudding for dessert.

MAXIMILIAN: With raisins.

JOAQUIN: I love raisins.

ADAM: I like my bread pudding without raisins. That's how my mother always made hers.

FELIPE: Bernarda Alba strikes me as the kind of a woman who uses raisins.

(Joaquin takes out a small book and writes something in it.)

TOMAS: Why? 'Cause she is so dried up?

FELIPE: What used to be a grape is now a prune.

TOMAS: Raisin.

MAXIMILIAN: Not like our beauty last night.

TOMAS: Shh.

JAIME: Shh.

MAXIMILIAN: Paca la Roseta.

TOMAS: You should never call a whore by her full name.

MAXIMILIAN: She wanted it from all of us.

FELIPE: Did she have a choice.

(The men laugh and pat each other on the back.)

MAXIMILIAN: I was the second to go at her. So she was still moist, but not a puddle.

FELIPE: When I got her it felt like a mud pie . . .

MAXIMILIAN: What a whore she is.

JOAQUIN: What whores you all are?

TOMAS: Men are forceful and take what they can.

MAXIMILIAN: That's right.

JAIME: Way of the world.

JOAQUIN: Really?

MAXIMILIAN: You think differently.

JOAQUIN: Yes.

MAXIMILIAN: That's because . . .

TOMAS: We don't want to fight.

JOAQUIN: She didn't want to share anything with you.

MAXIMILIAN: She did.

JOAQUIN: She has to. Economics. You are the whores for forcing her.

(They all laugh.)

FELIPE: A woman like that needs it in her all the time.

ADAM: Can't get enough.

MAXIMILIAN: That's right.

JOAQUIN: No, it isn't.

FELIPE: A pussy is a pussy.

JOAQUIN: Did you enjoy watching each other?

FELIPE: I kept my eyes on her tits.

JOAQUIN: Really?

MAXIMILIAN: Me on her legs.

TOMAS: You were done quick.

MAXIMILIAN: No I wasn't. I wanted to put it all over her face, but . . .

JOAQUIN: Real men like all their seeds inside the woman so children can grow.

MAXIMILIAN: I'm a real man.

JOAQUIN: Pepe . . .

MAXIMILIAN: Yes?

JOAQUIN: Lets it all fall in.

MAXIMILIAN: How do you know?

JOAQUIN: Because he went first . . . before I had a chance to realize what was really going on. And it took him a long time. He filled her.

TOMAS: We all filled her.

MAXIMILIAN: I was second and I played her slowly, like a guitar.

FELIPE: No you didn't.

MAXIMILIAN: Yes I did.

FELIPE: I have eyes.

MAXIMILIAN: You are full of shit.

(They are about to fight.)

TOMAS: If you put your tongue to it, there is no juice.

MAXIMILIAN: What? A pomegranate?

TOMAS: No, Bernarda Alba's prune.

(The men laugh.)

JOAQUIN: She'll hear us.

FELIPE: We deserve lunch after all this praying.

TOMAS: Yes, we do. That's what wakes are for. A little crying, a little "He was such a great guy," then stuff yourself.

JAIME: Absolutely. Praying, crying, wine, and a meal.

JOAQUIN: But we buried him already, it is not a wake.

ADAM: It's a meal after the wake.

JAIME: She's going to make us a delicious lunch. An omelet . . . giant with potatoes and onions, olives, tomatoes, and bacon. Believe me. I know her kind. Has to keep up appearances.

ADAM: Of course.

TOMAS: Yes, appearances.

FELIPE: Why won't she let us in.

MAXIMILIAN: She's afraid of her virgins.

TOMAS: Virgins my ass.

FELIPE: You've gone too far now.

TOMAS: I have to express myself.

JAIME: Her daughters are either too homely to be fucked . . .

MAXIMILIAN: Or too old to be fucked.

ADAM: Or too crazy to be fucked.

FELIPE: I've fucked crazy, old, ugly pussies. My prick sees a hole and up it goes.

(The door opens. Poncia enters; she is a big, round woman in her fifties. She holds a pitcher of lemonade.)

MAXIMILIAN: Is it up now?

FELIPE: No, but if I . . . tried. Put my mind to it . . .

JOAQUIN: Really?

PONCIA: It's like a cattle farm.

TOMAS: What, the smell?

PONCIA: It drips with fragrances.

TOMAS: It's hot out here. We've been sweating for half an hour.

PONCIA: Yes, the smell of bulls.

TOMAS: We waited patiently. Even though we were sweating to death . . .

ADAM: Waiting.

JAIME: For the ham.

FELIPE: Or the lamb.

TOMAS: And the potato omelet. I always dreamed of a real big woman like you suffocating me into ecstasy.

(Poncia laughs.)

PONCIA: Wash your mouth out with soap.

TOMAS: I made you laugh.

PONCIA: You've made me shake inside.

TOMAS: Meet me in the barn.

PONCIA: I'm in mourning.

(Poncia laughs.)

TOMAS: Then why are you not crying?

PONCIA: Because. I cried enough for my husband when he died. May he rest in peace. There is no water left in my eyes.

TOMAS: How about your boss?

PONCIA: Let his wife and his daughters mourn him. He was always trying to get some in the kitchen.

TOMAS: Don't tell Bernarda.

PONCIA: Never satisfied. That man satisfied her, but didn't satisfy himself.

JAIME: Your boss?

PONCIA: All men.

(She laughs.)

TOMAS: Fill my glass.

(Poncia does.)

PONCIA: Who else needs more?

(All the men lift their glasses.)

One at a time.

MAXIMILIAN: That's what she said last night.

PONCIA: Paca?

MAXIMILIAN: Were you listening at the door?

PONCIA: No.

MAXIMILIAN: Then how would you know?

PONCIA: I have a third eye.

MAXIMILIAN: What?

PONCIA: I read minds.

MAXIMILIAN: Then you must know that I'm thirsty.

(Poncia pours him lemonade.)

JOAQUIN: You read minds.

PONCIA: When I want to.

JOAQUIN: Try.

PONCIA: I don't want to.

(She pours him some lemonade.)

You like being thirsty.
JOAQUIN: No.
PONCIA: Yes.

(She laughs.)

JOAQUIN: Is Pepe El Romano expected here this afternoon?
PONCIA: Why would he be expected here?
JOAQUIN: He was at the mass.
PONCIA: He wasn't invited.
MAXIMILIAN: What's this obsession with Pepe, Joaquin?
JOAQUIN: I have to find Pepe El Romano, he said there might be an extra job guarding the sheep.
JAIME: Really?
TOMAS: I need a job.
ADAM: I'll do anything.
JAIME: I have four starving little girls. They want bread. They want bread.
FELIPE: Who doesn't.
TOMAS: Where is it? The job.
JOAQUIN: Thank God I can harvest my mind.
MAXIMILIAN: 'Cause you got a job! Come on, you punk, tell me about it.

(Maximilian punches Joaquin.)

JOAQUIN: One job for me.
TOMAS: Some guys got all the goddamn luck. Goddamn! *(To Poncia)* Excuse me.
PONCIA: No . . . I like to hear a good goddamn come out of a hungry man.
FELIPE: Are we going to get food?
JAIME: Or not!

PONCIA: Not even wine, only lemonade.

MAXIMILIAN: Doesn't she have any sense of morality?

PONCIA: I'm sorry.

MAXIMILIAN: Tradition.

PONCIA: She's steel.

MAXIMILIAN: Doesn't she want to honor her husband?

PONCIA: She thinks she is by saving him money even after death.

TOMAS: It wasn't his money.

PONCIA: She is honoring both her husbands. A widow twice; now that's a lucky woman.

JAIME: We came for no reason.

TOMAS: Well, pour some more. I hope this one is sweeter.

PONCIA: She rations my sugar. I am sorry. Believe me, I know how to make lemons sweet.

TOMAS: I bet you do!

PONCIA: I should have been a gypsy girl and danced with a tambourine . . . hitting inside my legs roughly, with my sweat coming down my thighs . . .

TOMAS: I'd lick it.

PONCIA: You dirty old man.

TOMAS: You like it, though.

PONCIA: I like to see you looking . . . hungrily. My mother always said let them look, we are not rich . . . but don't let them touch without . . .

TOMAS: Buying?

PONCIA: Without the holy sacrament.

TOMAS: I'll confess, then you give me communion.

PONCIA: Without the sacrament of marriage.

TOMAS: I have a wife.

PONCIA: I know, she's inside.

TOMAS: Having lunch.

PONCIA: Doing the rosary.

(*Tomas drinks his lemonade.*)

TOMAS: You've been a widow too long . . . Too long . . .

MAXIMILIAN: And your mistress?

PONCIA: Bernarda?

TOMAS: Yes.

PONCIA: Dry like a desert.

TOMAS: See?

PONCIA: And proud of it.

JOAQUIN: Proud?

PONCIA: But me, still moist . . . Let me fill your glass. I have to go get another pitcher.

FELIPE: Steal more sugar for me.

PONCIA: I'll do what I can.

JOAQUIN: Leave the woman alone.

FELIPE: Why?

JOAQUIN: She is doing her job.

PONCIA: Joaquin, you are right, if you wait here Pepe will show up. He went to take his mother home. I wish God would have made me a better liar.

JOAQUIN: How do you know he'll be back?

PONCIA: He is drawn here like a magnet to steel.

TOMAS: Why won't she let us in?

PONCIA: She is afraid you'll dirty her floor.

TOMAS: Or her mattresses.

PONCIA: She rules over her domain.

MAXIMILIAN: A woman must always listen to a man.

JOAQUIN: Not anymore.

PONCIA: Not anymore, what a sweet sound.

(Poncia laughs and exits.)

MAXIMILIAN: That's the trouble with this whole anarchist way of thinking. That's what's gone wrong in the world. If we are all equal. Women think they don't have to obey us. They think they can sit inside the house while we burn. That's the problem. How can we be equal? We have a prick and they have a hole. And a spear is what you need to conquer the world.

JOAQUIN: Those women in there are not anarchists.

ADAM: What are they then?

JAIME: Catholics, righteous, virginal.

JOAQUIN: Bourgeoisie.

(Pepe El Romano, who has entered unnoticed, speaks.)

PEPE: And rich. And in power.

TOMAS: What?

PEPE: They have taken our power.

MAXIMILIAN: I can push any woman down and fuck her into submission.

PEPE: Money is a better weapon than a prick.

JOAQUIN: Pepe, I'm ready to work.

(All the men surround Pepe and try to get Joaquin's job.)

MAXIMILIAN: I'm stronger than this wimp.

TOMAS: I'm an old man. I deserve a future, my limited future. Ten more years of work, that's all.

FELIPE: My mother was an orphan, my father died when I was two . . .

MAXIMILIAN: If you get me the job Paca will . . .

TOMAS: I'm an old man . . .

ADAM: I'll work twenty-four hours . . .

JAIME: You know I knew your father. I got your father to meet your mother, give me . . .

TOMAS: I'm—

JOAQUIN: Leave him alone, he offered it to me. His word of honor and honor still means something to Pepe El Romano.

PEPE: Someday. I'll be able to offer all of you jobs.

TOMAS: Sure you will.

MAXIMILIAN: Right.

FELIPE: Like she's offering us bread pudding.

JAIME: At this point, I'd be happy with a piece of bread with olive oil on it.

ADAM: And garlic.

FELIPE: You are making my mouth water.

(All the other men agree.)

PEPE: Tonight we will talk about it.

TOMAS: About the job, about how we can find some kind of work.

PEPE: No . . . about how if we all united as men and a country we could, we could be a force. If we didn't let the rest of the world treat us like dogs with fleas. We could show them. We are Spanish after all. We discovered The Americas. We ruled the world and we will do it again. Tonight at the tavern we will meet. Talk about the future. There is a plan and if we follow it, we will be conquerors again. Agreed?

JOAQUIN: Unite how?

PEPE: Become strong.

JOAQUIN: The mind or the body?

PEPE: So we can beat the shit out of anybody.

JOAQUIN: Through ideals?

PEPE: No. With our fists, with our guns. People want to take food from our table. If they want to take food from our table, we can slice their balls off.

JOAQUIN: We can build a world where there's food for everybody.

PEPE: Impossible.

JOAQUIN: Believe me.

PEPE: Sometimes you sound like a girl.

(The men laugh.)

JOAQUIN: Go ahead, laugh. But I use my mind before I use my fist.

PEPE: How about your balls?

MAXIMILIAN: Yeah, the balls.

JOAQUIN: I got a pair, so what?

FELIPE: But are they ripe? With fruit?

JAIME: All my balls have given me is more kids to feed.

MAXIMILIAN: Mine have given me hours of pleasure.

(Maximilian goes up to Joaquin.)

JOAQUIN: Leave me alone.

MAXIMILIAN: Joaquin, you are no longer fourteen.

JOAQUIN: None of us are.

FELIPE: I'm thirsty.

(Pepe throws them a large sack of wine.)

PEPE: Get drunk.
FELIPE: Thank you for this wine.
PEPE: There's more on my horse.
JAIME: And we can have it.
PEPE: I brought it for the wake.
MAXIMILIAN: You are my kind of man.
TOMAS: One hell of a guy.
JOAQUIN: Salt of the earth. That's how you want to be seen?
PEPE: A man who takes care of himself and his people.
JOAQUIN: Then listen to me. The anarchists believe that only if we
   live communally can we . . .
PEPE: Not until you have a drink.
JOAQUIN: But.
PEPE: Get drunk for christ's sake!

(Joaquin takes a big drink.)

JOAQUIN: That was sweet.

(Joaquin drinks again.)

PEPE: Get drunk. Good, because today we will soothe, we will wipe
   tears from their faces. Their father has died. How many women
   are in there?
TOMAS: About thirty.
PEPE: About thirty crying, kneeling, praying. In black. Longing,
   wishing. Their hearts breaking, calling out, to God, who is a
   man like us after all. There is nothing that sets me on fire more
   than a woman crying, kneeling, needing comfort. I'm sure God
   feels the same way, that's why he answers women's prayers more
   than men's. There is nothing more tempting on his earth than
   a woman needing the strong arm of a man. A woman wanting
   a man to engulf her . . . so she can drown in his strength. A girl

who needs a man's hand to wipe away her tears. Is the closest we come to heaven on earth. If you are lucky enough to be that man . . . A woman can only feel safe when a man has surrounded her. And today I am that lucky man.

(Pepe knocks on the door.)

TOMAS: No, we are supposed to stay outside.
PEPE: Never do what you are supposed to do. That's what my father taught me. So how many, six, five?
TOMAS: You know.
PEPE: I want to hear the number.
TOMAS: Five.
PEPE: Five sisters. Five sisters, a house with five sister and no man. Is a dried field ready for a match!

(Pepe knocks again.)

TOMAS: You can waste your time courting 'cause you got a goddamn job.

(Poncia comes to the door.)

PONCIA: Yes? I had to find the key for the cabinet where the sugar is kept . . .
PEPE: I want a drop.
PONCIA: Pepe . . .
PEPE: The first drop of something in that house that has been kept under lock and deep below.
PONCIA: No.
PEPE: No?

(We see one of the shutters open, it is Adela.)

And what are those eyes by the window?
ADELA: Adela's green eyes.
PEPE: Green like pine needles?

ADELA: Like alligator skin.

PEPE: Emerald green?

ADELA: Like a deep river or lake.

PEPE: Or a field of grass.

ADELA: Where you can rest your head and dream.

FELIPE: You said there was more wine?

PONCIA: Adela, leave the window.

ADELA: No.

PONCIA: I don't want to get into trouble.

ADELA: Then go back inside and be my mother's servant.

PONCIA: Don't you dare talk to me like that.

ADELA: Give me a moment.

PONCIA: In a moment the world can explode.

ADELA: Not if you've been raised right.

PONCIA: What?

ADELA: If you've been raised right, it takes years before anything explodes.

PONCIA: Well.

ADELA: And you raised me right.

PONCIA: Did I?

ADELA: Better than my mother could have.

PONCIA: Are you trying to flatter me?

ADELA: You know I speak my mind!

PONCIA: I taught you that.

ADELA: I know.

PONCIA: I'm proud.

ADELA: I might be the baby, but I am stronger than all the rest of them . . .

PONCIA: Don't compete with your sisters.

PEPE: There is no competition.

PONCIA: Do not fall for his flattery.

ADELA: Don't worry.

PONCIA: All right, but if you are not back in five minutes . . .

ADELA: I will be.

PONCIA: My sweetie, my favorite, my student.

ADELA: Mamá.

PONCIA: Shh. If your mother heard that I'd be out of here fast.

ADELA: My teacher, then.
PONCIA: Baby, what a beautiful baby you are . . .

(Poncia exits.)

ADELA: From you I learned to grab in an instant and think later.
PEPE: Good lesson.
ADELA: That's what the working class is for. That's why they bathe us
and make us breakfast. To bring us down to earth.
TOMAS: The wine?
PEPE: Is on my horse in the field.
MAXIMILIAN: And we can drink.
PEPE: Drink.
FELIPE: How much?
PEPE: Drink it all.
TOMAS: Everything?
PEPE: All. Everything. Satisfy yourselves.

(All the men, except for Joaquin and Pepe, run out to the field.)

ADELA: They all admire you.
PEPE: Yes.
ADELA: Why?
PEPE: There's a stallion in your barn.
ADELA: Yes.
PEPE: You should study him.
ADELA: Why?
PEPE: So you can learn about me.
ADELA: I will when everyone is sleeping.
PEPE: Good.
ADELA: I love you.
PEPE: How can you prove it to me?
ADELA: I will learn how to ride a horse.
PEPE: Stallion.
ADELA: Stallion.
PEPE: Ride but not tame?
ADELA: I want to scream.

PEPE: I will make you scream.

ADELA: A scream from deep inside, past my soul. A scream that comes from somewhere deeper than my soul.

JOAQUIN: Then read.

ADELA: What?

JOAQUIN: About utopia. Utopia, a place where we are all equal.

ADELA: I don't want to be equal.

JOAQUIN: It's the only way to find that scream you are looking for.

ADELA: How do you know?

JOAQUIN: You want to be free?

ADELA: Of all this.

JOAQUIN: It's not between his legs.

ADELA: You sound like my mother.

JOAQUIN: I want to be your equal.

ADELA: I want a man to conquer me.

JOAQUIN: You think that will set you free?

ADELA: From my mother.

JOAQUIN: This country is your mother.

ADELA: I want my will to be my own, not hers.

PEPE: I will make you mine.

ADELA: Pepe, Pepe, Pepe!

PEPE: Good. Now go.

ADELA: Yes, what ever you say, whenever you say it.

(She closes the shutters and leaves.)

PEPE: That's what a man wants from a mistress.

JOAQUIN: What?

PEPE: A girl who wants a free will is a girl who will give you herself.

JOAQUIN: Free will is what a man wants for a country.

PEPE: No, profits, money, land . . . That's a country. That's what family is all about.

JOAQUIN: She has no money.

PEPE: I know.

JOAQUIN: So how can she give you power?

PEPE: She can give me life. Her life underneath me. Living for me.

JOAQUIN: I see. I understand.
PEPE: What?
JOAQUIN: Who you are becoming.
PEPE: You don't like it?

(A shutter opens. We see Angustias's eyes.)

The brown eyes of my beloved.
ANGUSTIAS: Hazel, actually.
PEPE: Ever changing.
ANGUSTIAS: True to you.

(She opens the door and walks out. She is old, thin, and stiff.)

PEPE: My wife.
ANGUSTIAS: Not yet.
PEPE: I'm young.
ANGUSTIAS: I know.
PEPE: I want it now.
ANGUSTIAS: I'll tell her soon.
PEPE: When is soon?
ANGUSTIAS: You are so eager.
PEPE: To hold you in my arms.
ANGUSTIAS: I thought it was over for me.
PEPE: A woman your age is perfect for a man like me.
ANGUSTIAS: I wish I would have met you when I was twenty.
PEPE: When you were twenty I was seven.
ANGUSTIAS: I love you.
PEPE: Yes.
ANGUSTIAS: A house, a field, and you. That's all I want.
PEPE: So when is soon?
ANGUSTIAS: Today.
PEPE: Yes.
ANGUSTIAS: I don't want her to hold on to my inheritance.
PEPE: And without a husband she will.
ANGUSTIAS: But a husband I will have.
PEPE: Yes.

ANGUSTIAS: Oh, yes.

PEPE: Me.

ANGUSTIAS: You.

PEPE: Oh yes me, all of me.

ANGUSTIAS: Thanks to my guardian angel.

PEPE: Which sent you to me?

ANGUSTIAS: I know. I was out sitting, waiting for confession. And out you came. It had been a long confession.

PEPE: I prayed longer so I could see you again.

ANGUSTIAS: One look . . . and I knelt by you and I knew. And my pride melted. That's love. Isn't it? Pepe. Isn't it love. Melting pride, suspicion, remorse. All of that. All that is the worst parts of me. What I had become. You made it all melt. It's true love. It is, isn't it?

PEPE: Do you want me to get on my knees again?

ANGUSTIAS: Once was enough.

PEPE: Good.

ANGUSTIAS: But I want you to sing by my window with a guitar about love not fulfilled.

PEPE: Love not fulfilled.

ANGUSTIAS: So my sisters can feel . . .

PEPE: Envy?

ANGUSTIAS: Their lot in life.

(Poncia runs in.)

PONCIA: Your mother is calling for you.

ANGUSTIAS: So?

PONCIA: If she finds you here with two men.

ANGUSTIAS: Two?

JOAQUIN: Yes.

ANGUSTIAS: I didn't notice you.

JOAQUIN: I'm the planet that orbits the sun.

PEPE: I'm the sun.

JOAQUIN: Yes. Aren't you?

(Pepe laughs.)

ANGUSTIAS: You are.

PONCIA: Come in before she finds you.

PEPE: I am impatient.

ANGUSTIAS: For what?

PEPE: To be inside, to reach your soul.

ANGUSTIAS: I am a Catholic you know.

PEPE: I met you at confession.

ANGUSTIAS: It is so tempting. But if I waited forty years. I can wait. God, how long can I wait?

PEPE: That's why the marriage has to be soon.

ANGUSTIAS: I'll talk to her now.

PEPE: Tonight, ten guitars.

ANGUSTIAS: I adore you.

(Angustias closes the shutters and exits.)

PONCIA: Joaquin, get him out of here.

PEPE: Soon, you too will be mine.

PONCIA: I don't belong to anyone.

(Poncia exits.)

JOAQUIN: Both things in one house.

PEPE: Clever.

JOAQUIN: The conquering Roman.

PEPE: That's my name.

JOAQUIN: But Rome fell.

PEPE: I won't.

JOAQUIN: There are people who believe in no man controlling anyone, no woman being controlled. People being allowed to formulate their own rules and order, not church, not force . . .

PEPE: Do you hate me because of it?

JOAQUIN: What?

PEPE: My maleness.

JOAQUIN: No.

PEPE: No?

JOAQUIN: What color are my eyes?

251

PEPE: Black.

JOAQUIN: Like two dark holes.

PEPE: Yes.

JOAQUIN: And if you look into them you will drown.

PEPE: Never.

(Pepe takes Joaquin's face and looks into his eyes.)

What color are mine?

JOAQUIN: Brown.

PEPE: Like the earth.

JOAQUIN: And they will bury people like me.

(Joaquin looks away.)

PEPE: You looked away.

JOAQUIN: Yes.

PEPE: Who's stronger?

JOAQUIN: You are.

(Pepe lets go of him.)

PEPE: Good.

JOAQUIN: For now.

PEPE: Forever.

(The men run in. They are drunk.)

JOAQUIN: I won't let it be forever.

TOMAS: Drank all the wine.

MAXIMILIAN: Every drop, God bless you.

TOMAS: Now if we could only eat the earth.

PEPE: I have jobs for you.

TOMAS: You do.

PEPE: I want three guitarists.

MAXIMILIAN: My guitar is with my horse.

TOMAS: I'm a better guitar . . .

JAIME: I also played, I helped your father . . .

ADAM: I can spin a tune that will make her swoon . . .

PEPE: I can only afford three.

TOMAS: Me. I am telling you . . .

MAXIMILIAN: I'm getting my guitar.

(Maximilian runs out.)

PEPE: I'll hold an audition.

FELIPE: I can play the castanets.

PEPE: I want the best three guitarists in town.

FELIPE: Goddammit, I never learned how to play the guitar.

TOMAS: And you call yourself Spanish.

FELIPE: What good are guitars without castanets?

TOMAS: He only wants guitars.

FELIPE: Goddamn. Goddamn, goddamn!

TOMAS: Hey, careful, she can still hear you.

FELIPE: Who?

TOMAS: Bernarda Alba.

FELIPE: Fuck her. Fuck the whole fucking world.

TOMAS: Get some booze into him and he forgets his manners.

FELIPE: Why not castanets?

PEPE: Your bad luck.

JAIME: Do you need singers?

ADAM: I can sing; sang in the choir.

PEPE: I will decide after the audition

TOMAS: I'm the best guitarist around here. I helped Bernarda Alba's first husband serenade her.

PEPE: So?

TOMAS: I'm not auditioning, just give me the job.

PEPE: Did you get better with age or worse?

TOMAS: Better. Of course better. When you get older you don't worry about showing off. You disappear in the chords.

(Maximilian appears with his guitar.)

MAXIMILIAN: I'm ready to prove myself.

TOMAS: Youth.

PEPE: This better be good.

MAXIMILIAN: These fingers are magic fingers.

PEPE: Magic, I like that.

MAXIMILIAN: Then magic you will get, boss.

TOMAS: Youth pushes too hard.

JOAQUIN: What?

TOMAS: It's a quiet thing.

JOAQUIN: Playing?

TOMAS: Life.

JOAQUIN: Maybe.

TOMAS: I'm sure of it.

JOAQUIN: You are.

TOMAS: Yeah, I am.

(Maximilian strikes a chord.)

MAXIMILIAN: I have to tune it. Damn.

PEPE: Take your time.

MAXIMILIAN: Thank you.

TOMAS: See, he's complicating things. Simple. Keep everything simple.

JOAQUIN: But not politics.

TOMAS: Even that.

JOAQUIN: Not if war breaks out.

TOMAS: Even then.

JOAQUIN: I don't agree with you. A man has principles. I believe anarchism will save me. So I have to be willing to save it and . . .

MAXIMILIAN: I want it quiet for my audition.

JOAQUIN: And shout my beliefs.

TOMAS: Let's pay attention to the man.

PEPE: I am ready.

(Maximilian plays wonderfully. Everyone applauds warmly.)

MAXIMILIAN: Who ever thought a hobby would come in so handy?

PEPE: What makes you think you got the job?

MAXIMILIAN: The competition applauded.

PEPE: But I didn't.

MAXIMILIAN: You didn't like it?

PEPE: I'm not saying that.

FELIPE: Let me try.

MAXIMILIAN: You play the castanets.

FELIPE: I think I got a gift.

MAXIMILIAN: All right.

(Maximilian hands Felipe the guitar.)

FELIPE: Is it still in tune?

MAXIMILIAN: What difference will it make in your hands?

ADAM: Give the man a chance.

(Felipe starts playing; his playing is weak.)

PEPE: Sorry.

JAIME: All right, my turn.

MAXIMILIAN: So my guitar is everybody's guitar.

JOAQUIN: Isn't that great?

MAXIMILIAN: Not if they cheat me out of a job.

JOAQUIN: They won't. He wants three guitarist.

MAXIMILIAN: You got a point.

(Jaime takes the guitar. He plays and sings well.)

JAIME *(Sings)*:
     Sweet canary
     Sweet canary
     In your cage
     I will feed you
     Little sweeties
     You will sing
     You will sing
     Just for me

>Little darling
>Little darling
>In your cave
>I will feed you
>Sweet caresses
>You will love me
>You will love me
>Love just me

PEPE: Hmm.

JAIME: Not bad.

PEPE: I might have found two guitarists.

MAXIMILIAN: So I got the job.

PEPE: You might.

MAXIMILIAN: My luck is turning, my luck is changing.

JOAQUIN: By lending your guitar.

MAXIMILIAN: Why don't you become a priest?

JOAQUIN: What?

MAXIMILIAN: You are always looking for the good in things. And you don't even enjoy a good gang-bang.

JOAQUIN: I read.

TOMAS: So I'm the other guitarist.

PEPE: If you prove yourself.

TOMAS: You are going to make me audition?

PEPE: Past glories don't impress Pepe El Romano.

TOMAS: Loan me the guitar.

MAXIMILIAN: It might need tuning by now.

(Tomas grabs the guitar. He plays and sings astonishingly well.)

TOMAS *(Sings)*:
>Age
>Is not bitter
>Age
>Resounds with
>Hope.

Age
Doesn't stop
You
It lets you
Let go.

And you know
That a dark street
Is dangerous and sweet.
You know
That starvation is
Always
Waiting at your feet.

And you know that all that's out there
On the streets
Are lizards and reptiles and wild boar and geese.

Age
Is not bitter
Age resounds with
Hope.
Age doesn't stop
It lets you let go.

Age
Doesn't mean the
Feast is over
Age only means
It's getting late.
So,
Just let it play.

PEPE: Well, well, well!
TOMAS: It's got soul.
PEPE: And I need to buy soul.

TOMAS: To tame.

PEPE: The richest lady inside that house.

ADAM: She's old. You are going to try to marry Bernarda Alba.

JOAQUIN: No, Angustias.

ADAM: You are a better man than me.

FELIPE: Or smarter.

JOAQUIN: Or cunning.

TOMAS: I will rent you my soul.

PEPE: You got the job.

TOMAS: How much.

PEPE: Depending on how it works, I'll tip you generously.

FELIPE: I can sing.

PEPE: We will all sing.

ADAM: You'll pay us all to sing.

PEPE: The singers will get lunch at the tavern, the guitarist a fee.

(The men yell and thank Pepe.)

JOAQUIN: She wanted a song of love unrequited.

PEPE: You must know one, Tomas?

TOMAS: Well, usually I sing about happiness and fulfillment.

MAXIMILIAN: So do I. Why depress people?

FELIPE: Joaquin used to write songs.

PEPE: That's right. About butterflies caught in a net.

MAXIMILIAN: Little butterfly . . .

PEPE: Write me one.

JOAQUIN: I don't know.

ADAM: That's right. He called them poems.

PEPE: Go to the tavern and order lunch.

TOMAS: God bless you.

JAIME: Amen.

PEPE: Tell them Pepe El Romano and the brown shirts are paying.

TOMAS: Ever since you were a little boy I knew you were the one.

PEPE: The one?

TOMAS: That would lead us out of the hell hole.

JAIME: I just want to be sure. One of the other two guitarists is myself, me.

MAXIMILIAN: And me.

PEPE: Of course.

MAXIMILIAN: Thank you.

JAIME: God bless you.

FELIPE: Lunch, we are finally going to eat lunch.

ADAM: A big omelet with potatoes and sausages.

PEPE: That's only the beginning. We need jobs. Men need jobs before anybody else. Before women for sure.

TOMAS: For sure.

PEPE: Spanish men need jobs, before Africans for sure?

ADAM: Goddamned Moroccans.

TOMAS: You are right.

PEPE: Do you think our king cares if we have jobs or not?

FELIPE: He does not give a goddamned.

PEPE: The Brown Party does. It cares. It wants us to unite. Do you think the French care?

TOMAS: They are across the border and they want our ass.

PEPE: And the Latin-Americans, liberated themselves from our tyranny. They knew how bad things were going to get.

FELIPE: Fucking Cubans.

MAXIMILIAN: Do not forget the Filipinos.

PEPE: And the U.S. of A.

TOMAS: And Paraguay, Argentina, Peru . . .

JAIME: Stop it! Stop it! And even little Puerto Rico. It's too long a list.

TOMAS: Too long.

PEPE: We have been betrayed by everyone.

TOMAS: Goddamn it, nobody cares about us. Motherfuckers.

PEPE: If we unite. If we say no to loose thinking. No, women cannot work. No, marriage cannot be a contract to be broken . . . if she feels like it.

JOAQUIN: What are you talking about?

PEPE: That's what the anarchists want. If a woman is not happy she can break the marriage contract. Not sacred vows, but contract.

TOMAS: But women are always not happy.

FELIPE: Not happy, always.

PEPE: They want to take the power away from the male. I say give the power back to the cock of the walk.

TOMAS: That's right. Give me back my cock. Poverty has taken it away from me. When I was a young boy, I ruled by force. By the force of my manhood. By the hope I felt between my legs.

PEPE: It's still there.

JOAQUIN: The key idea of anarchism is simple: true emancipation can only be brought about by the direct action of those concerned, the workers themselves, and not under the banner of any political party or ideological body. The anarchist idea and the true emancipatory revolution can never be brought to fruition by anarchists as such but only by the vast masses.

PEPE: There are no longer any peaceful solutions. War has been declared and the government has been the first to proclaim itself belligerent . . . The government does not waste its time swatting flies; it rushes to destroy anything that might constitute a defense of Spanish civilization.

JOAQUIN: Property is theft. The passion to destroy is an obsessive passion.

PEPE: Men need to be told what to do.

JOAQUIN: Do you?

PEPE: Well.

JOAQUIN: Do you.

PEPE: I'm a self-made man.

JOAQUIN: And they're sheep.

PEPE: They have to speak for themselves.

JOAQUIN: But you have more rights than they do.

JAIME: Is that what you're telling us, you think you are better than me? 'Cause you spent all day seducing virgins. I have to feed my four daughters . . .

PEPE: I came to offer you a way to work.

TOMAS: And you have.

PEPE: Go have lunch.

(The men go, each thanking Pepe as they leave.)

JOAQUIN: The Brown Shirts are fascists.

PEPE: They are going to put this country back on track. No more
    kings, no more anarchist . . .

JOAQUIN: Only thugs?

PEPE: Are you going to write me that song?

JOAQUIN: Love unrequited?

PEPE: Yes.

JOAQUIN: And what do I get paid?

PEPE: The poet?

JOAQUIN: The lyricist.

PEPE: A chance to write about me.

(Pepe sits on the bench.)

Read to me.

(Joaquin takes out his book and reads aloud.)

JOAQUIN:

    Crocodile eyes peek through windows
    Are underneath veils.
    They cry crocodile tears.
    They lie about their age for years.
    They soothe all your fears.
    They are a young girl's flirting glance
    They are a woman's secret weapon.
    They are what you want.

    Why do I love you
    When you are everything I hate.
    Why do I think it's too late for caresses.
    Crocodile eyes.
    I don't have crocodile eyes.
    No danger, no temptress am I.

    Why do I love you
    When you are everything I hate?

(Pepe walks away.)

> You will destroy me.
> It will be too late.
> Crocodile eyes.
> Why don't I have crocodile eyes.
> No danger, no temptress am I!

Is that unrequited or jealous.

(One of the doors swings open and Maria Josefa, the grandmother, enters. She is dressed in the style from decades ago. She wears a lot of necklaces and bracelets. And heavy make up.)

MARIA JOSEFA: Young man? Do you have a parasol?

JOAQUIN: I'm afraid I don't, Maria Josefa.

MARIA JOSEFA: You know my name.

JOAQUIN: You are famous around here.

MARIA JOSEFA: For my beauty.

JOAQUIN: For being the matriarch of this huge house.

MARIA JOSEFA: No, my daughter Bernarda is the matriarch. I am the beauty. She always hated me. It must be hard for a daughter to have her mother be more desired than she. Do you have a parasol? I don't want the sun to ruin my white skin.

JOAQUIN: Maybe you should stay inside the house.

MARIA JOSEFA: Never, they are all suffocating in there. Never! Do you hear me?

(She goes inside and does not close the door, comes out another.)

> I need to breathe
> Air.
> I need to fly
> My arms upright
> I need to swing my hips around a man.

(She goes up to Joaquin and holds him.)

I need a child
to milk from me!
I need to scream!

Aaah
Oooh
Eeeh.

PONCIA: Maria Josefa, come back here. You cannot go out. Your
   daughter will kill you.
MARIA JOSEFA: I'm free!

(Poncia goes to her. Maria Josefa is wild with energy.)

I'm free. I'm me! A woman! Yes!

(Amelia enters.)

PONCIA: Amelia, come out here and help me.
MARIA JOSEFA: I want. I want. I want.

(Maria Josefa walks toward Joaquin seductively.)

JOAQUIN: You're free?
AMELIA: I'm afraid to go out there.
PONCIA: Help me!
AMELIA: There's a man out there, what if Mamá sees me?
PONCIA: Stop being so spoiled.
AMELIA: Grandma, come inside the house.
MARIA JOSEFA: Come out here with me and let's dance with this
   man.
AMELIA: He's a peasant, Grandma.
MARIA JOSEFA: If they know how to work the fields, they know
   how to love a woman.
PONCIA: Get out of here.
MARIA JOSEFA: No!

(Joaquin leaves.)

He is gone.

AMELIA: Time to go inside for a nap.

MARIA JOSEFA: I wanted a party.

AMELIA: We must stay inside and suffer.

MARIA JOSEFA: No.

AMELIA: We must cry and repent.

MARIA JOSEFA: No.

AMELIA: That's our lot in life, Grandma.

(They start going inside. Poncia begins to close the doors. The women are gone.

Joaquin sneaks back in; he writes and reads.)

JOAQUIN: Time to go inside for a nap. I want a party. We must stay inside and suffer.

(Blackout.)

Act Two

Night. The field. Pepe is with Adela. He is in his underwear. He is trying to take off her dress.

PEPE: Why do you always wear this green dress?
ADELA: It's lurid.

> *(Joaquin walks in with Pepe's clothes. He drops them and exits. They do not notice him.)*

PEPE: I do not want you to be lurid.
ADELA: Why not?
PEPE: 'Cause you are mine.
ADELA: I am.
PEPE: Prove it.
ADELA: I am only lurid for you.
PEPE: Yes.
ADELA: It's how I lost my virginity. To you, with you, in you.
PEPE: No, I was in you.
ADELA: My tongue.
PEPE: Yes?

ADELA: Was inside of you, wasn't it?

PEPE: Yes.

ADELA: It's green like a crocodile.

PEPE: Really? Your tongue.

ADELA: My exterior.

PEPE: Ahh.

ADELA: I hope it makes me strong.

PEPE: What.

ADELA: An outside coating.

PEPE: Take it off.

ADELA: Armor.

PEPE: My love.

ADELA: No.

PEPE: Now.

ADELA: I don't want you to marry her, my own sister. The one I've
always hated.

PEPE: I have to.

ADELA: But why her?

PEPE: Shh.

ADELA: Why?

PEPE: Money.

(He starts to unbutton a few buttons.)

ADELA: No.

PEPE: I need to touch the skin. Your skin.

ADELA: I want to be protected.

PEPE: No such thing.

ADELA: You and I . . .

PEPE: I know . . . I know.

ADELA: We . . .

PEPE: We?

ADELA: Are. We are. We are.

PEPE: I'm lying to myself, I know.

ADELA: You do?

PEPE: It's you I want.

ADELA: It is?

PEPE: Yes.

ADELA: Say it.

PEPE: It's you I want . . . yes.

ADELA: Say it again.

PEPE: It's you I want and love . . . yes.

ADELA: Say it again.

PEPE: It's you I lust for, want, and love . . . yes. You are.

ADELA: Then cancel the wedding.

PEPE: No.

ADELA: Why not?

PEPE: She has things I need.

ADELA: But love comes first.

PEPE: But her lands are what I need.

ADELA: How about what I need.

PEPE: You're young.

ADELA: So.

PEPE: She's old.

ADELA: What do you mean.

PEPE: I'll kill her.

ADELA: What?

PEPE: One child from me will kill her.

ADELA: No. You're wrong.

PEPE: No, I'm not.

ADELA: You don't know her, she has a will like my mother. My mother had me when she was her age and she's still here. Demanding, asking. Repressing. Someone like Angustias lives forever.

PEPE: I'm going to marry her. End of this discussion.

ADELA: I'll do something crazy.

PEPE: Give me what's mine.

ADELA: What?

PEPE: Lie down with me in the barn now. Or never again.

ADELA: Really?

PEPE: Yes.

ADELA: Never again.

PEPE: I'll never touch you again.

ADELA: I love your touch.

PEPE: I know you do.

ADELA: Your lips.

PEPE: My lips I save for you.

ADELA: You'll never kiss her?

PEPE: Only politely on the forehead.

ADELA: Really?

PEPE: Really.

ADELA: She'll want more.

PEPE: She'll do what I tell her to do.

ADELA: Your mouth is mine.

PEPE: Yes.

ADELA: I believe you.

PEPE: You should.

(They kiss.)

ADELA: I'm weak.

PEPE: That's why I love you.

ADELA: You love me?

PEPE: Of course.

ADELA: Love me and the baby.

PEPE: What?

ADELA: The baby.

PEPE: What are you talking about?

ADELA: The baby we made. The one that's inside of me.

PEPE: No.

ADELA: I can feel it. Us.

PEPE: Not my baby.

ADELA: What?

PEPE: Not mine.

ADELA: Who else?

PEPE: Joaquin's.

ADELA: What?

PEPE: Joaquin.

ADELA: Joaquin is the only man around here that has never looked at me with hunger. Joaquin? Are you crazy. You are a liar.

PEPE: I do not lie.

ADELA: You do. You know it's only you.

PEPE: Come here goddamn it. Joaquin!

(Joaquin walks in.)

ADELA: You were watching.

JOAQUIN: Yes, he tells me to.

ADELA: Oh, my God.

PEPE: You heard it all.

ADELA: He watches from so close. And I can't feel your eyes.

JOAQUIN: He can.

PEPE: He always watches. I always feel him.

JOAQUIN: That's how he traps me. By trapping you.

PEPE: I'm a good hunter.

JOAQUIN: Since childhood. He does . . . I watch and think. Think that I can get away. That this ideology will free me or religion will. Or a moment of peace. But he always comes along with something tempting. It's something in his heart that destroys me, but makes me come to life again. Do you understand?

PEPE: Shut the fuck up.

JOAQUIN: I've seen it all.

ADELA: Good.

JOAQUIN: Good?

ADELA: Then you know it's his baby.

JOAQUIN: Yes.

ADELA: Good. You see, Pepe?

JOAQUIN: Only he has been with you.

ADELA: My witness.

PEPE: But you would say it was yours for me.

JOAQUIN: I don't know.

PEPE: You would.

ADELA: No, you won't.

JOAQUIN: I don't know.

PEPE: Yes. Goddammit, say yes!

JOAQUIN: We have to be quiet.

PEPE: That entire house is snoring.

JOAQUIN: You never know.

PEPE: Believe me, it is.

JOAQUIN: You never know.

ADELA: I will not bear a bastard.

JOAQUIN: It already is.

ADELA: I will say it was born premature. You marry me tomorrow, conceived on the same night. It's been done before.

PEPE: Never.

ADELA: I'll make you pay.

PEPE: I have to marry her, then kill her with love, that's the plan.

ADELA: But I'm not willing to go along with it.

PEPE: You better be.

ADELA: I have my own free will.

PEPE: I hate that about you.

ADELA: You do? Strange, because it's what brought me here to you, to this moment. What created the child inside me. If you marry my sister . . . I will betray you. I'll tell her what's inside of me. And she will cut you off. She won't used anything that any of us have had before. Not even a towel to wash her face with.

(Adela starts to exit.)

PEPE: Come back here.

ADELA: No.

PEPE: Obey me.

ADELA: No.

(Adela exits.)

JOAQUIN: Free will is a dangerous thing.

PEPE: Shut up.

JOAQUIN: Caught in your own trap.

PEPE: You fucking . . .

(Poncia enters.)

PONCIA: You're going to wake her up.

PEPE: No, they're all asleep. I can hear it.

PONCIA: So sure of yourself.

PEPE: Why not?

PONCIA: You thought I was . . . and I'm not.

PEPE: What?

PONCIA: Asleep.

JOAQUIN: That's true.

PONCIA: One eye always open, that's me.

JOAQUIN: We know.

PONCIA: I know you do. But the others, too much maleness in their veins to see the other side.

JOAQUIN: You really think that?

PONCIA: Yes.

JOAQUIN: You see the difference in me.

PONCIA: Since you were a baby. Now take him home.

JOAQUIN: Pepe.

PEPE: Yes.

JOAQUIN: Poncia is right, it's late.

PEPE: It's never too late to serenade.

PONCIA: What?

PEPE: Serenade.

PONCIA: At this hour.

PEPE: I'm a man of whim. I go with my whims. *(Calling out)* Maximilian.

(Maximilian rushes in.)

PONCIA: They all wait for you now.

PEPE: Yes.

(Joaquin starts to lay Pepe's clothes out on a bench.)

PONCIA: What has the world come to.

PEPE: Impressed.

PONCIA: No.

PEPE: You should be.

PONCIA: Men will follow anything, every woman knows that. Put out a scent and they start licking their lips.

PEPE: True.

MAXIMILIAN: We are his army.

PONCIA: Bunch of thieves.

PEPE: Get Tomas.

MAXIMILIAN: We are going to serenade now?

PEPE: That's right.

JOAQUIN: Now. You're pushing.

PEPE: Don't tell me that I'm pushing.

JOAQUIN: You are pushing her to . . .

MAXIMILIAN: It's midnight.

PONCIA: Past midnight.

PEPE: So we can enter their dream world.

PONCIA: Bernarda Alba will not like this.

PEPE: So what?

PONCIA: She already has doubts about your intentions. And well she should.

PEPE: But her daughters don't.

PONCIA: Poor girls. That's what happens when you shelter your children from the world.

JOAQUIN: What?

PONCIA: When the world attacks, they explode.

PEPE: I'm in command here now.

MAXIMILIAN: Yes, sir.

PONCIA: They watch. All the women in that house. They see you coming. A mile away. They can smell you.

PEPE: Including you?

PONCIA: I have a third eye. I know your every move.

PEPE: I see.

PONCIA: You should be careful with people's souls.

PEPE: Why?

JOAQUIN: Because sometimes they are fragile.

PONCIA: Sometimes they seek revenge.

PEPE: What?

PONCIA: They destroy themselves, so they can destroy you.

PEPE: Not me.

PONCIA: You never know.

(Poncia starts to exit.)

PEPE: Where are you going?
PONCIA: To pretend that I'm asleep.
PEPE: Oh.
PONCIA: So you can wake me up.
PEPE: I see.
PONCIA: So I can continue the lie.
PEPE: The lie.
PONCIA: Of what I know and what I hear in the dark.
PEPE: I see.
PONCIA: Even I protect you.

(Poncia exits.)

JOAQUIN: I wish I could destroy you with my vengeance.
PEPE: Help me get dressed.

(Joaquin starts to help Pepe get dressed.)

Good boy.
JOAQUIN: I believed in something. Purity.
PEPE: I'm not pure.
JOAQUIN: I know.
PEPE: Good.
JOAQUIN: And yet, now I follow you around like a dog.
PEPE: Yes. You do.
JOAQUIN: What once was full inside of me, is now a sea of tidal waves inside my chest.
PEPE: How did I do it?
JOAQUIN: Never mind.
PEPE: I want to know.
JOAQUIN: No.
PEPE: I want to know your soul.
JOAQUIN: You do?
PEPE: Yes.

JOAQUIN: Well . . .

PEPE: Tell me. How I've shattered your soul.

JOAQUIN: When I saw how you can love her.

PEPE: Adela.

JOAQUIN: Yes.

PEPE: Jealous.

JOAQUIN: Yes, I am.

PEPE: Good.

JOAQUIN: For you.

PEPE: I don't love Adela.

JOAQUIN: Yes. You do. You do. I know that you do.

PEPE: I take her.

JOAQUIN: That's all?

PEPE: Put all my will into taking her.

JOAQUIN: It resembles love.

PEPE: Love is something you save for your mother and your children.

JOAQUIN: Why not take me?

PEPE: I have.

JOAQUIN: How? How have you taken me? In my sleep?

PEPE: You were once going to be a poet. Now you only write songs for me. You were once going to change the world. Now you are only happy when you are watching mine.

JOAQUIN: I only see you.

PEPE: Because of my strength.

JOAQUIN: Because of my weakness.

(The men enter.)

TOMAS: All I can tell you is that Paca is very disappointed.

JAIME: I already had her.

ADAM: Me, too.

FELIPE: But I hadn't.

PEPE: She'll wait. She's the kind that waits.

TOMAS: What do you want, boss?

MAXIMILIAN: I told you, he wants us to play the guitar.

TOMAS: Again?

PEPE: Work is something you do every day, not just on a whim.

TOMAS: Right.

PEPE: You playing guitars for me is now work.

TOMAS: Yes, sir.

FELIPE: And singing is lunch still? A free lunch at the tavern?

PEPE: Yes.

ADAM: I'm going to have sausages this time.

FELIPE: Again?

ADAM: Yes. The Brown Shirts are the way.

PEPE: They make your belly full.

ADAM: Yes, they do.

MAXIMILIAN: Indeed.

PEPE: Yes.

MAXIMILIAN: And anarchism is still bullshit.

TOMAS: And we got to put an end to it, right?

PEPE: Joaquin?

JOAQUIN: Just sing.

ALL *(Singing)*:

> Mm-mm mm-mm mm-mm mm-mm
> Song bird, song bird, song bird, song bird
> Song bird–song bird
>
> Song bird, song bird, just out of reach
> Sweetheart, song bird
> Hear me beseech of a love
> I really feel
> But it's not quite your ideal
> So all my songs, you steal,
> You sing my songs

JOAQUIN: I wrote that about you.

PEPE: For me, not about me.

JOAQUIN: I'll stay quiet.

ALL *(Singing)*:

> Song bird, let me cling as I fall
> Sweetheart, don't deny me my call
> Honey bee
> Though you sting me be sweet
> Sing back to me, my honey bee
>
> Be my sweetheart hear me sweetheart
> Song bird, song bird
> Love, not your ideal
> But come near
> Feel that it's real
> This is real

TOMAS *(Singing)*:

> Love is not bitter,
> Love resounds in hope
> Love does not stop you,
> It lets you let go

ALL *(Singing)*:

> Song bird, song bird, song bird

> *(During the song Bernarda's house has illuminated again. Poncia runs in.)*

PONCIA: It's too late, Bernarda Alba said go home.

PEPE: But my heart.

PONCIA: Your heart can wait.

PEPE: Can it?

PONCIA: Yes.

PEPE: Really?

PONCIA: Absolutely.

TOMAS: Why?

MAXIMILIAN: Yes, why?

FELIPE: A man's heart is tender.

ADAM: Tender like a sausage.

JOAQUIN: Sneaky like a tarantula.

JAIME: Watch it, punk.

JOAQUIN: Even now, sometimes I hear my own voice and it comes flying out.

PONCIA: You proved your point, get out of here.

TOMAS: Love knows no time. It's out of time, courageous, like you. Timeless. Love feeds on the unexpected . . .

JAIME: So do children.

FELIPE: So do singers.

ADAM: Sausage I'm getting.

TOMAS: His heart felt it. What's time? When the heart feels it.

PEPE: Yes.

(Angustias runs in.)

ANGUSTIAS: Yes. I was awake anyway, every day. I can't sleep. I won't sleep till I sleep . . . with a ring on my finger . . . and your arm around my waist. And your maleness suffocating me till I can not breathe.

JOAQUIN: Till you drown.

ANGUSTIAS: Till I drown in your sweat, Pepe. Pepe! And I am born again a woman, not a virgin. A mother, not a spinster.

PEPE: Baby, baby, baby. Let's do it before the wedding night.

ANGUSTIAS: I want you to respect me.

TOMAS: He will. You've proved it enough. How many weeks have we sung for you?

MAXIMILIAN: Eight.

JAIME: Eight, every night. I've grown calluses.

FELIPE: I've had a lot of lunches.

(Adela opens the shutters of her door.)

ADELA: And I . . .

ANGUSTIAS: Have longed to be in my shoes.

ADELA: No?

ANGUSTIAS: In my bed.

PONCIA: Girls, your mother wants you inside.

ANGUSTIAS: In his arms?

ADELA: Yes, in his arms.

ANGUSTIAS: Long for it.

ADELA: I will. If I imagined it right. He can only live in my imagination. Right?

ANGUSTIAS: Die longing for it.

JOAQUIN: No.

ADELA: What?

JOAQUIN: Run to me.

ADELA: To you.

JOAQUIN: Yes. I am safe.

ANGUSTIAS: Sister, a declaration of love, don't turn it down.

ADELA: Only pity.

PEPE: Isn't pity love?

PONCIA: Never.

TOMAS: I don't know, I pitied my wife, that's why I first asked her to dance with me.

JAIME: I asked my wife out 'cause she had crooked teeth. I thought if she has crooked teeth, she will never smile for another man.

FELIPE: And was it true?

MAXIMILIAN: No.

JAIME: What are you saying?

MAXIMILIAN: She smiled. With her lips closed, that's even more inviting.

ADELA: When are you marrying him?

ANGUSTIAS: Tomorrow. Whether Mother approves or not.

ADELA: And if I tell you . . .

ANGUSTIAS: That he really loves you?

ADELA: Yes. That he touched me. That he taught me how to hide. That he bruised me. That I died and then grew a tough exterior where no one can get in! Not sister, not mother, only him. See, it's green. The texture of crocodile. No sweet rose in me, sister.

ANGUSTIAS: I won't believe you.

PEPE: Good, there you see a wife.

ADELA: Look at me and see the spiteful bitch I have become.

ANGUSTIAS: Because envy and greed have turned all of you against me. You are only my half-sister, not whole. I had to live with your father after he married Mamá. I had to see all of you get born and use some of the money that was mine. Your father didn't have a penny. He just knew how to mount Mamá. She paid for him with my father's money.

ADELA: And now . . .

JOAQUIN: She's going to do the same thing.

ANGUSTIAS: I'm going to give into joy.

PONCIA: Joy?

ANGUSTIAS: Awful word in this country, "joy."

PEPE: And I can give it to you.

ADELA: Joy.

ANGUSTIAS: Yes sister, happiness.

JOAQUIN: And I can share it with you, Adela.

ADELA: How?

JOAQUIN: I'll teach you how to think.

ADELA: I don't want your pity.

JOAQUIN: I'm willing to give you my mind.

ADELA: Killer.

PEPE: What?

ADELA: You are a killer.

PEPE: All hunters are.

ADELA: I will . . .

PEPE: What?

PONCIA: Haunt you.

PEPE: No.

(Adela exits.)

PONCIA *(To Pepe)*: Your will be done.

ANGUSTIAS: God's?

PONCIA: Sure, God's.

(Poncia exits.)

ANGUSTIAS: You are not going to stay and chaperone me.

TOMAS: We will.

JAIME: All of us.

MAXIMILIAN: Want to hear music?

FELIPE: I'm a baritone.

ADAM: Me, tenor.

MAXIMILIAN: Sweetly, that's how we wanted to reach you. With sweetness, with the smell of lilacs and carnations. We wanted you to smell that as we played.

ANGUSTIAS: And I did.

PEPE: It made you young?

ANGUSTIAS: Eighteen.

PEPE: I can make you feel like you are eighteen.

ANGUSTIAS: Yes.

PEPE: That's a good quality in a man.

TOMAS: The best.

PEPE: You know. I think I love you for that.

ANGUSTIAS: That's why the music is so tender.

PEPE: You find me tender.

ANGUSTIAS: A lost boy.

PEPE: I . . .

(He takes her away from the men.)

I think I am.

ANGUSTIAS: And I will baby you.

PEPE: I'm safe.

ANGUSTIAS: Yes.

PEPE: Thank you.

(Tomas walks toward them.)

TOMAS: We wanted our chords to penetrate through the tissues of regret to the loveliness that is inside you.

ANGUSTIAS: The woman in me. Yes. The woman in me. A frightened child, looking for her father in every man's eyes, but trained not to look at any man straight in the eyes. Trained not to long for anything . . . I want to look at all of you.

PEPE: Line up.

TOMAS: What?

PEPE: So she can look at you.

(The men line up: Adam, Felipe, Maximilian, Jaime, Joaquin and Tomas.)

ANGUSTIAS: What's your name?
ADAM: Adam, like the first one of us.

(She looks at him.)

ANGUSTIAS: Shy? I didn't know men were shy.
ADAM: We are not.
ANGUSTIAS: The eyes do not lie.
FELIPE: Felipe. I'm resourceful, aggressive.
ANGUSTIAS: Look at me.

(Felipe tries.)

Don't look away. Scared.
FELIPE: Yes, I confess I am.
ANGUSTIAS: So am I.
PEPE: Do we need to continue this?
ANGUSTIAS: I'm having fun. Maximilian, the guitar player.

(Maximilian plays and looks at her.)

MAXIMILIAN: Yes.
ANGUSTIAS: Full of fire.
MAXIMILIAN: All artists are.

(Joaquin laughs.)

PEPE: Shh!
JAIME: Jaime, I helped your father court your mother.

(Angustias looks at him.)

ANGUSTIAS: I love your pride.

JAIME: Thank you, m'am.

JOAQUIN: Joaquin, it rhymes with gasoline.

ANGUSTIAS: I can't look at you.

JOAQUIN: Please do.

ANGUSTIAS: No.

JOAQUIN: Come on, I am your mirror.

(He takes her face.)

ANGUSTIAS: Let me go.

PEPE: Let her go.

JOAQUIN: Look at me.

ANGUSTIAS: Please, Pepe.

JOAQUIN: Why not?

ANGUSTIAS: I only see longing.

JOAQUIN: Something that we share.

PEPE: Enough of this.

ANGUSTIAS: Now there's you.

PEPE: What do you see?

ANGUSTIAS: Happiness. Hope. A future.

TOMAS: The eyes can lie.

PEPE: Go to hell.

TOMAS: That's why I never looked a woman straight in the eyes. And
     I'm not starting now.

ANGUSTIAS: So you are the only one left?

TOMAS: Yes, but no thank you.

ANGUSTIAS: For ten pesetas?

TOMAS: For ten pesetas?

ANGUSTIAS: Right in your hands, right now.

TOMAS: Ten pesetas.

ANGUSTIAS: Yes.

TOMAS: So you can look right into me?

ANGUSTIAS: Yes.

TOMAS: The ten pesetas first.

ANGUSTIAS: Give him the money.

(The doors fling open and Maria Josefa enters, screaming.)

MARIA JOSEFA: My baby. She did it. My baby! The fruit is swinging from the tree!

ANGUSTIAS: Oh God, what is she raving about now. Grandma!

MARIA JOSEFA: She did it! She had the strength to do it! My baby! Born from me! Men. Why are there men here? Men! All young! All waiting! All of them wanting me. I can smell them. No! I am not ready for admirers. Not today.

ANGUSTIAS: So old, so vain.

TOMAS: Look into my eyes. I need the ten pesetas.

ANGUSTIAS: She's mad, you know that? Grandmother, you are senile. Do you know that?

MARIA JOSEFA: You are too bitter to be a granddaughter of mine.

ANGUSTIAS: I better get Poncia.

PEPE: Come back out.

ANGUSTIAS: I'll try.

MARIA JOSEFA: I am alone. And you all want me. I should pray!

PEPE: Well, here you are Maria Josefa. Alone . . .

MARIA JOSEFA: Alone. Yes!

PEPE: With the men. At last.

MARIA JOSEFA: My baby. Child of winter, my daughter was too old. So I gave birth to her. My poor baby.

(She cries. The men laugh.)

TOMAS: Quiet! She was a grand lady. Beautiful, white, soft skin . . .

MARIA JOSEFA: She gave me back spring. How could she. No, baby! I need a man to comfort me!

(Maria Josefa runs toward Tomas, he holds her. Poncia enters.)

PONCIA: Come with me.

MARIA JOSEFA: No!

PONCIA: Right now!

MARIA JOSEFA: I need a man to comfort me.

JAIME: Let us help.

PONCIA: You are not welcome in that house.

MAXIMILIAN: Right.

FELIPE: Bitches.

PONCIA: Maria Josefa, come with me!

MARIA JOSEFA: No, I need a man to comfort me.

PONCIA: Amelia, come help me!

TOMAS: Here I am. Feel the strength in my arms.

MARIA JOSEFA: You are like an oak.

TOMAS: Lean on me.

MARIA JOSEFA: Water is dripping from her veins, mineral water from the mountains where we come from. Where our roots are planted. My poor baby . . . We should have gone to the seashore. It's not hot there. The sea cools the skin . . .

(Amelia is now there in her nightgown.)

AMELIA: Why is it always me?

MARIA JOSEFA: Do you want to go to the seashore, young man?

TOMAS: Young?

MARIA JOSEFA: Young to me.

AMELIA: Let's go, Grandma.

MARIA JOSEFA: Jealous, aren't you?

AMELIA: Not tonight.

MARIA JOSEFA: What makes this night different?

PONCIA: Silence.

AMELIA: I know. I am silent. I am being silent!

MARIA JOSEFA: His arms are strong.

AMELIA: Grandma, there is bread pudding inside.

ADAM: Really?

FELIPE: Shh.

MARIA JOSEFA: For me?

AMELIA: Yes.

JOAQUIN: Why are your eyes so red?

AMELIA: Tears.

PONCIA: Of remorse.

AMELIA: Stop with your opinions!

MARIA JOSEFA: Come and play the guitars by my window. I'll escape through the window. And we will go away. By the seashore. The sea cools the skin. The skin cools the soul and the foam will revive us.

TOMAS: Yes. I'll bring my guitar and play you songs of happiness and joy.

MARIA JOSEFA: Yes. How sweet men are.

AMELIA: Please, come now!

MARIA JOSEFA: Yes! To the seashore, children. To the seashore!

(Maria Josefa walks toward Amelia.)

AMELIA: Yes, Grandma.

MARIA JOSEFA: It will revive us.

AMELIA: Please, Grandma. Come.

(Amelia starts to cry.)

PEPE: Hysterical women.

(Amelia and Maria Josefa have exited.)

PONCIA: Hysterical, really? That's what you think?

PEPE: Yes.

PONCIA: Get ready to face hell! Hell is coming to you.

(Poncia exits.)

PEPE: How? Hysterical women. A house full of insane women.

TOMAS: Girls do crazy things for love, they follow you around with a knife, they set themselves on fire, they stop eating.

JOAQUIN: So do men.

TOMAS: Really?

JOAQUIN: Yes.

MAXIMILIAN: I don't believe that.

FELIPE: Neither do I.

ADAM: I never have done anything crazy. Not one of us.

JOAQUIN: How do you know?

FELIPE: Can you prove it?

JOAQUIN: Yes.

JAIME: How?

JOAQUIN: I have. I have done insane things for love.

MAXIMILIAN: For the love of a woman?

JAIME: Of course for the love of a woman.

ADAM: What else is there to love?

JOAQUIN: No! For that man. *(He points at Pepe)* Pepe El Romano, Rome has conquered us again.

TOMAS: You mean you admire him?

JOAQUIN: I know that inside of him are a hundred yellow butterflies that want to fly. But he keeps them pressed, suffocating against the pages of a book, a book called fascism.

PEPE: Sometimes when I look into your eyes they fly.

JOAQUIN: Really?

PEPE: Sometimes I see you walking towards me. I feel like running and putting my arms around you.

JOAQUIN: Then why don't you?

PEPE: Training.

JOAQUIN: The church?

PEPE: My training is the only solid thing I have.

(Poncia and Angustias enter.)

PONCIA: Adela . . .

JOAQUIN: Yes.

PEPE: She told her. She got her revenge. Good. She deserved it. If the woman loves me, she'll forgive me.

PONCIA: She didn't say a word.

PEPE: No?

PONCIA: She used an action instead.

PEPE: What?

PONCIA: She found a gesture more potent than words.

PEPE: What?

ANGUSTIAS: Adela has hung herself.

(The men for once have nothing to say. They sit, silent.)

JOAQUIN: How?

PONCIA: With the linen from her bed.

ANGUSTIAS: The virginal bed.

JOAQUIN: No.

PEPE: Yes.

ANGUSTIAS: My mother said she died a virgin.

JOAQUIN: She gave . . .

ANGUSTIAS: My mother knows the truth. My mother sees everything. She died a virgin. Poor thing.

TOMAS: Yes. Poor thing.

ANGUSTIAS: I will not.

PEPE: Never.

MAXIMILIAN: Poor thing. Deprived. From joy.

FELIPE: Yes, the joy of a man.

ADAM: The only real joy. The joy of a child.

PONCIA: Springing forth.

MAXIMILIAN: Yes.

TOMAS: The things that go in. The things that go out. The fluids. That's life.

JOAQUIN: Poncia!

PONCIA: I could see it with my third eye, she died a virgin.

PEPE: And tomorrow we will marry.

JOAQUIN: Poncia, that's a lie.

PEPE: Yes, marriage. Angustias, our bodies united, a family, beginning.

JAIME: Some joy in tragedy.

FELIPE: Amen.

ADAM: Will you be having a meal?

PEPE: For the wedding, not the wake.

ANGUSTIAS: Suicides don't get buried.

MAXIMILIAN: Purgatory forever.

FELIPE: Eternity.

PEPE: Angustias, at first I didn't love you . . . But with time I have grown to need the calmness of your breath. And the assurance of your walk. And it has taken me to love.

ANGUSTIAS: I do not forgive you.

PEPE: For what?

ANGUSTIAS: For it not being at first sight.

(The women exit. Joaquin closes the doors behind them.)

TOMAS: Funerals are becoming more and more common, a month of death. First the father, now the daughter. She loved her father, that's for sure. Makes me want to live.

JOAQUIN: She will haunt you.

(Pepe slaps him across the face.)

JOAQUIN: She is haunting you already.

PEPE: In a new society there is no past.

JOAQUIN: Boys, let's come up with a song for this moment, a lament for the lost of innocence. I'll do the words, you the tune.

PEPE: It's too late.

MAXIMILIAN: Let the poet speak.

ADAM: Yes. Please.

(Adam goes and gets the guitars.)

PEPE: Have your say.

(Joaquin takes out his book and looks through it. Then he puts it on his forehead.)

JOAQUIN *(Spoken)*: Adela died late Friday night, she hung herself.

> Oh, Adela
> Oh, Adela
> Oh, lost soul.
>
> My darling girl, I hope they put
> water lilies on your grave, like Ophelia,
> she was also betrayed by love.

(The men start to play something on the guitars.)

MEN *(Singing)*:
> Adela died late Friday night.
> Oh, Adela
> Sweet Adela
> Oh.

PEPE: No music for those words.
TOMAS: Why?
PEPE: Because they are bleak and I want joy.
JOAQUIN: Joy?
PEPE: Why not. That's what money in your pocket is for, joy.
TOMAS: No music.
MAXIMILIAN: No music, fine.
ADAM: But let him speak it.
JAIME: Yes, Pepe?
PEPE: Speak it.

(The men sit silently; they look at Joaquin, who continues to speak to Pepe.)

JOAQUIN:
> Adela,
> I want to believe
> that really, you drowned yourself
> in the warm waters of a river.
> Not by hanging
> in the stillness of the air.
> Sleep well.

PEPE: So do I.
JOAQUIN: Why? It's you that killed her.
PEPE: Lust . . .
JOAQUIN: Yes.
PEPE: Is a man's right.
JOAQUIN: Even if it kills the other person?

PEPE: Get him.

(They run after Joaquin. Tomas watches.)

JOAQUIN: Blood is on your hands, Pepe. More blood. Pepe. Pepe. Pepe!

(The men get Joaquin.)

PEPE: Spread his legs.
MAXIMILIAN: Are you sure?
PEPE: Yes.
TOMAS: He was your friend.
PEPE: So?
TOMAS: One of us.
JOAQUIN: You killed her with your lies.

(Maximilian grabs Joaquin by the hair and throws him on the bench.)

MAXIMILIAN: He is not a liar.
PEPE: I am not a liar.
    Spread his legs.

(They do.)

    Turn him around so his ass is facing me.
TOMAS: Wait a minute.
PEPE: Do it.
MAXIMILIAN: Can you do it?

(They turn him around.)

PEPE: My gun up your ass! Isn't that what you always wanted?

(Pepe puts the gun near Joaquin's ass.)

JOAQUIN: No! I wanted you.

PEPE: Aren't you scared?

JOAQUIN: No.

TOMAS: No?

FELIPE: No?

MAXIMILIAN: Why?

JOAQUIN: Why!

PEPE: Yes, why.

ADAM: You are going to die.

JOAQUIN: Pepe, do you not know that words live forever?

PEPE: No, they don't.

JOAQUIN: Yes, they do!

TOMAS: Pepe, wait a minute, I think he's right.

JOAQUIN: Forever!

(Pepe cocks his gun.)

PEPE: I can't do it.

(Pepe puts the gun down by Joaquin. Adam and Felipe are still holding onto him. Jaime steps to the side. Tomas is still sitting on the bench.)

MAXIMILIAN: Why not?

PEPE: Because I love him.

MAXIMILIAN: You love him.

(Maximilian hits Pepe.)

JAIME: Coward.

MAXIMILIAN: Your country is ashamed of you. You love him.

PEPE: Let me run.

MAXIMILIAN: Away from him?

PEPE: Yes, away from him.

MAXIMILIAN: Faggot.

PEPE: No. I want a house, children, and peace. Let others win the war.

(Maximilian pushes Pepe again.)

Peace be with you, Joaquin.

JOAQUIN: And with you, Pepe.

> *(Pepe runs out. The men look to Maximilian. At first he doesn't know what to do. Then he picks up the gun, puts it on Joaquin's ass and cocks it.)*

MAXIMILIAN: I am the rooster here now.

> *(Blackout.*
>
> *In the darkness we hear the gun go off eight times. The men are illuminated only by the gun fire.*
>
> *Lights up.*
>
> *The men are rolling Joaquin down to the tip of the stage.*
>
> *Maximilian is playing the guitar.*
>
> *Tomas picks up Joaquin's book, puts it in his pocket, and walks away.*
>
> *Blackout.)*

END OF PLAY

EDUARDO MACHADO was born in Cuba and came to the United States when he was eight. He grew up in Los Angeles. He is the author of more than forty plays, including *The Cook, Havana Is Waiting, The Modern Ladies of Guanabacoa, Fabiola, In the Eye of the Hurricane, Broken Eggs, Once Removed, A Burning Beach* and *Stevie Wants to Play the Blues.* His plays have been produced at Seattle Repertory Theatre, the Goodman Theatre, Hartford Stage, Actors Theatre of Louisville, Mark Taper Forum, Long Wharf Theatre, Hampstead Theatre in London, American Place Theatre, Cherry Lane Theatre, INTAR Theatre, Theater for the New City, and Repertorio Español, among many others. Mr. Machado wrote and directed the film *Exiles in New York*, which played at the AFI Film Festival, South by South West, The Santa Barbara Film Festival and The Latin American International Film Festival in Havana, Cuba. He is a member of the Actors Studio, The Ensemble Studio Theater, and an alumnus of New Dramatists. His plays have been published by Theatre Communications Group and Samuel French.

Mr. Machado is Head of Playwriting in the Goldberg Department of Dramatic Writing at New York University's Tisch School of the Arts. *Tastes Like Cuba: An Exile's Hunger for Home,* a food memoir by Eduardo Machado and Michael Domitrovich, was released by Gotham Press in 2007. Mr. Machado has just completed two new plays, *That Night in Hialeah* and *Mariquitas.* He is also a writer on the HBO show *Hung.*